Structures for Writing the First Draft

Secondary Level

How to Create Analytical Paragraphs Through Critical Thinking

A Practical Plan for Writing the First Draft

Dr. Robert A. Pauker

Case studies and scenarios in this book do not reflect the behaviors or actions of any specific individual.

Structures for Writing the First Draft – Secondary Level, 3rd Edition
Copyright © 1988, 2004, 2015 Robert A. Pauker All rights reserved.

ISBN-13:   978-1514326268
ISBN-10:   1514326264

Table of Contents

Preface

Our current world is dominated by a series of short messages communicated through emails, Facebook, Twitter, and the like. The students of today believe that the brevity of these messages is a positive. The types of communication that have grown out of technology reduce clarity and heighten assumption. These students often become indignant at the idea of explaining their point of view with depth.

I began the Structured Writing and Thinking Program in 1984. At that time, I had been a consultant for a few years and had an opportunity to observe how students approached writing. I found that a sizeable group of students had difficulty organizing their paragraph responses. This organization was complicated by the philosophy of some teachers that students should just put down their thoughts in any order.

Coupled with these observations, I, also, was influenced by the investigation I was conducting in 1986 and 1987 for my book on critical thinking from the American Association of School Administrators, entitled Teaching Thinking and Reasoning Skills. From this experience, I began to draw a few conclusions that influenced key components of the Structured Writing Program. These are two of the most pronounced conclusions.

First, I came to believe that a highly structured writing approach did not get in the way of creative thinking. In fact, I found that creative and critical thinking work hand in hand. As the Structured Writing and Thinking Program evolved, I began to observe that students who learned this six-step process could comfortably infuse their "individual voices" into the structure; this meant that their personal styles of expression could be incorporated into their paragraphs or into parts of their stories.

Second, I realized that certain students had a more difficult time of organizing their thoughts than others. When given a sequence of steps that facilitated this organization, these students could produce high-quality paragraphs. I began to understand that there is a marked difference between "how one writes" and "what one writes." The structure minimizes the stress related to "how the student organizes the rough draft paragraph"; as a result, the student can devote his or her productive energies to "what is the content of my message."

The Structured Writing Program only centers on the composition of first draft paragraphs. Once this initial draft is completed, students can apply relevant skills and utilize the flow of their inner voice to make modifications. My observations indicated that a well-designed rough draft paragraph made this second phase of revision much easier.

Finally, I recognized that rough draft paragraphs need to be focused on one specific concept or idea. Writing a paragraph that began as follows: "There are many causes of the American Revolution." resulted in a relatively meaningless paragraph that only listed general ideas. A paragraph that began with a specific, centered main idea produced an analytical rough draft paragraph. For example, "The Colonial leadership refused to comprise on the Stamp Act, even though the British showed a willingness to make modifications."

Therefore, each main paragraph in the Structured Writing system is based upon one area of focus.

The idea of centering each paragraph on an area of focus became crystallized in my mind in the mid-1980s when I was consulting to an insurance company. I was brought in to work with the company's engineers who analyzed the condition and status for pieces of equipment that could cost millions of dollars. This analysis was necessary before the company could determine appropriate insurance rates.

These engineers had to write clear reports stating problems and recommendations related to these expensive machines. Clients and the actuaries of the insurance company read these reports. I was brought in to train the engineers to write clearer reports that were both analytical and logical.

What I found was training these engineers to create an area of focus for each paragraph of the report resulted in highly improved paragraphs. For example, one paragraph might center on the narrow focus of "pitting in the shell of the steam drum." Consequently, the reader understood the singular purpose of the paragraph.

I hope you have fun with this six-step Structured Writing process as you teach students the value of clarity and analysis in their writing.

Here are a few points to keep in mind when reading through the examples of this process.

1. Every paragraph is based upon a specific focus. The paragraph begins with "a main idea" and not "the main idea." There are many possible main ideas on which the paragraph may center, as opposed to one right main idea.

2. When writing the paragraph, each part of the six-step analytical process relates to previous parts. For example, the sentences in part two relate to the main idea stated in part one; the response to part three is based on the response in part two. As a result, the rough draft paragraph is very logical.

3. Success with this method is dependent upon the student understanding of the topic and the focus. The old adage "garbage in and garbage out" applies. The teacher can look at the student's sentences(s) for chapter one of this process and know immediately if the student comprehends the content or the topic.

When you teach the Structured Writing process, it is essential to spend time training students to become proficient with each step of the process. Here are a few points to keep in mind.

1. Take the student through the process step-by-step. Let the student complete the first step before describing the second.

2. Give students time to share their responses and an opportunity to borrow ideas from each other during the training phase. Have students read responses including previously completed steps. For example, after completing step three of the process, a student will share his or her sentence for steps one, two, and three.

3. Work with the students to embellish the quality of their responses. With content writing, insist on appropriate terminology.

4. Push students toward in-depth sentences that complement previously stated language but do not repeat.

5. Require that rough draft sentences be longer, except when writing a personal narrative. For example, I require that most rough draft sentences be, at least, twelve words; this encourages students to elaborate and to play with the inclusion of prepositional phrases or dependent clauses.

I hope you enjoy your experience with this process. I look forward to hearing how your students are doing, and I am happy to answer any questions as you put this process into play. Here is my email: c3pauker@gmail.com.

                                        Robert A. Pauker
                                        Ridgefield, CT

About this Book

This book explains The Structured Writing process by providing multiple annotated examples for literature, science, social studies and mathematics. In addition, the final section of this book demonstrates how to utilize The Structured Writing process to create a complete personal narrative essay.

The book is organized into these five parts.

Part 1 **Structuring a Response to Literature**
Samples of *persuasive, expository, poem analysis, personal narrative,* and *letter paragraphs*

Part 2 **Structuring a Response to Science Text, Article or Experiment**
Samples of *persuasive, expository, article, personal narrative,* and *business letter paragraphs*

Part 3 **Structuring a Response to Social Studies Text, Article, Video or Research Question**
Samples of *persuasive, expository, chapter text, personal narrative,* and *historical letter paragraphs*

Part 4 **Structuring a Response to a Mathematical Process or a Decision Based Upon Mathematics**
Samples of *persuasive, mathematical principle, article, personal narrative,* and *business letter paragraphs*

Part 5 **Writing a Personal Narrative Essay**

The annotated examples demonstrate how to apply each of the six steps of The Structured Writing process to a particular area of focus. The area of focus is the central theme or purpose of the paragraph. Analytical paragraph writing requires that this focus be specific in nature. The logical sequence of each step of the process provides students with a critical thinking structure that makes producing in-depth paragraphs easy.

The reader can begin his or her exploration in The Structured Writing process by reading the section of this book that is of most immediate interest. The teacher of science would most likely turn to Part 2 immediately; the teacher of mathematics would turn to Part 4 immediately.

> On a personal note, as you read each section think about how you can incorporate annotated examples into your daily instruction.

Introduction

What is the Structured Writing Process?

The Structured Writing process is an easy-to-use methodology that increases student communication, organization, and comprehension. This process becomes a cornerstone for all content areas. Teachers can infuse this process into direct instruction and into assessment. By engaging in the Structured Writing process students learn to reflect upon the meaning of key concepts. In addition, students become proficient at analyzing actions, events, and behaviors.

The Structured Writing process is comprised of six steps. Each step encourages students to explore an area of focus with greater depth. This exploration results in an investigation into the causes and impact of the focus. In essence, each step complements all previous steps and sets up the coherency and logic of what is to follow.

Structured Writing paragraphs can center on a multitude of focus areas, including the following:

- an explanation of the conclusion from a science experiment;
- an investigation into how an application of mathematical skills can result in a product beneficial to a certain group;
- an analysis of how character behavior leads to a character change;
- an exploration of how the behaviors of one group influence the actions of another group; and
- a personal reason for supporting a controversial issue.

Students can use the Structured Writing system to produce these paragraph types.

- expository paragraphs
- persuasive paragraphs
- personal narrative paragraphs
- paragraphs for a personal or business letter
- interpretive paragraph about a quotation or poem

Each of these paragraph types requires an in-depth analysis that pushes students to reflect about the learning or their experiences.

How Does the Structured Writing Process Support Accelerating Student Success?

Twenty-First Century Skills emphasize critical thinking, problem solving, and decision-making. The thinking involved in Structured Writing centers on all three of these areas. Each step of the process depends on the application of strong literal, inferential, and evaluative comprehension. Students are expected to center their paragraph development through a step-by-step analysis that addresses multiple causes or consequences, as well as an in-depth exploration of how one concept or idea influences other concepts or ideas.

The Structure Writing paragraph addresses the need for teaching writing within each discipline, as well as, applying writing skills to problem solving situations. Students gain proficiency in gathering and organizing relevant data/information, as well as how to apply the information towards a greater product.

Instructional practice must be devoted to the belief that students learn to evaluate behaviors and actions presented through the curriculum. This includes student proficiency in analyzing central ideas from multiple sources. The steps of the Structured Writing process facilitate student evaluation of literary, historical, and scientific behavior. Students learn to engage in meaningful exploration of how one action or behavior affects others and the influence of specific actions on central ideas, themes, and hypotheses. This in-depth reflective process enhances the likelihood of meaningful connections and logical explanations.

With these strategies, students gain proficiency in expressing a point of view and a comfort in persuading others to consider specific ideas. Students structure presentations in a logical manner. This logic is designed to match the audience and the type of message being delivered.

Students apply the Structured Writing process to communicate several instructional demands. Each analytical paragraph enhances comprehension and conceptual understanding. Here are a few examples of this connection.

- Explain how one event or action influences subsequent behaviors or actions.
- Analyze personal perspective and/or the perspective of others.
- Make connections among disciplines or between self and a significant concept.
- Evaluate information for in-depth analysis.
- Assess multiple interpretations.

Part 1

Structuring a Response to Literature

Students often are required to write responses to a specific type of focus. These areas of focus are designed to measure their ability to write about literary concepts, such as the following:

- Reactions to characters
- Analysis of a quotation
- Evaluation of a problem
- Ability to make connections

These types of responses can be difficult to organize. In order to simplify this task, the student can use this simple six-step process.

Step 1: main idea or stated reason
Step 2: for example
Step 3: why
Step 4: why of why
Step 5: why important
Step 6: as a result

This section contains examples of how the six-step process can be used with the types of focus areas in an English curriculum. Therefore, when required to write in-depth responses, students only need to remember the purpose of each step.

The simplicity of this process becomes valuable for students who are intimidated when writing on their own and during testing situations. By using these steps, students are no longer concerned about "how" to answer a question; they only need to center their energy on the best way to apply the content of the response into each of these six steps.

The examples in this section provide illustrations of these applications.

☞   **Keep this in mind:** Stay centered on one area of focus

Each of the applied responses that follow is based on the short story "A Mystery of Heroism" by Stephen Crane. The student would generate these paragraph responses after completing the reading and, if appropriate, the discussion.

Situation 1: Analyzing a Quotation

A student with average comprehension is asked to respond to this area of focus.

Focus: Select a quotation from the story and tell why the quotation is significant.

This student selects the following quotation.

"I ain't afraid to go. If you keep talking, I will go."

Step 1:

In this "main idea," the student describes when the quote was stated and the circumstances under which the quote was stated. The second (and third) sentence(s) of the main idea explain(s) the meaning of the quotation.

Main Idea   Collins (the main character) states these words to the other soldiers after they dare him to go out into the middle of the enemy rifle fire. This quote shows that Collins is very intimidated by his peers, and he really does not care to risk his life. In spite of this, he is determined to prove his manhood.

Step 2:

In the "for example," the student elaborates on the main idea with more detail. When editing the response, the student might cross out the words "for example" in order to improve word flow. However, it is better to use this lead in phrase during the process of elaboration because the student stays more centered on the purpose of each step.

For Example   For example, Collins realizes that his surroundings are very dangerous as he hears the shells exploding all around. He knows that taking the "dare" of the other soldiers would be foolish.

Step 3:

The student explains "why" this event took place. The explanation needs to have some level of depth showing that the student understands the theme of the story. The same premise holds for the "why of why" component. The student creates a question based on his or her response to the "for example." The question begins with the word "Why." This question for Step 3 includes a word or phrase from the "for example" response.

"Why" Question   Why does Collins do this even though he realized it is foolish?

Why   Collins, actually, brings the situation onto himself when he announces to the troops that there was bound to be water in the old well.

Step 4:

The student asks another related "why" question using a word or phrase from the most recent sentence.

"Why" Question   Why did he announce this to the troops?

Why of Why   In a stressful situation like war, people are looking for a relief from the stress of worrying about death. Collins provides the men with this relief the moment he shares his interest in finding out if there really is water in the well.

Step 5:

The "why important" requires the student to tell the significance of the quotation. In addition, he chooses to create some type of connection. This connection can be to other literature, history, or personal experience.

Why Important   This quotation is important because the words show his actual reluctance to be pushed to do something that is so dangerous. However, there is not way out. Collins reminds me of the character of Goober in the novel The Chocolate War by Cormier who is intimidated by the Vigils to unscrew the desks.

Step 6:

In the "as a result," the student describes the consequences of the connection and relates the connection to the speaker of the quotation.

As a Result   As a result, Goober acts so that his peers will like him, even though they really are making fun of him. Similarly, Collins decides to get the water from the well so that his peers will not mock him.

By writing these six parts continuously, the student has created an in-depth rough draft response that meets these criteria.

- The response is analytical.
- The response focuses on the quotation.
- The response explains the relation of the quotation to the theme of the work.
- The response is organized.
- The response makes a valid connection, if appropriate.

The total response looks like this. The final draft response is divided into two paragraphs because of length.

Student Paragraph

Collins (the main character) states these words to the other soldiers after they dare him to go out into the middle of the enemy rifle fire. This quote shows that Collins is very intimidated by his peers, and he really does not care to risk his life. In spite of this, he is determined to prove his manhood. For example, Collins realizes that his surroundings are very dangerous as he hears the shells exploding all around. He knows that taking the "dare" of the other soldiers would be foolish. Collins, actually, brings the situation onto himself when he announced to the troops that there was bound to be water in the old well. In a stressful situation like war, people are looking for a relief from the stress of worrying about death.

Collins provides the men with this relief the moment he shared his interest in finding out if there really was water in the well. This quotation is important because the words show his actual reluctance to be pushed to do something that is so dangerous. However, there is no way out. Collins reminds me of the character of Goober in the novel The Chocolate War by Cormier who is intimidated by the Vigils to unscrew the desks. As a result, Goober acts so that his peers will like him, even though they really are making fun of him. Similarly, Collins decides to get the water from the well so that his peers will not mock him.

Situation 2: Reacting to a Story

A student with average comprehension is asked to respond to this item.

Tell about your initial reaction(s) to the story.

Step 1:

In the "main idea," the student describes his or her initial reaction and whether that reaction changed. The student, also, explains what part of the plot led him or her to this reaction.

Main Idea	My first reaction is to pity Collins because he cares so much about what the other soldiers think. Collins has to risk his life in order to prove his worth to himself. However, my reaction of pity changes to respect by the middle of the story. It is doubtful if the men who bullied him to act would have had the courage to stop and assist the dying soldier in the middle of the battle field.

Step 2:

In the "for example," the student elaborates on the main idea with more detail. When editing the response, the student might cross out the words "for example" in order to improve word flow. However, it is better to use this lead in phrase during the process of elaboration because the student stays more focused.

For Example	For example, Collins' first reaction to the dying man shows a frightened soldier who does not want to help. Then, his actions are those of a hero who grants the dying man his final wish, even though Collins might lose his life.

Step 3:

The student explains "why" he or she reacted this way. The explanation needs to have some level of depth which shows the student understands the theme of the story.

"Why" Question	Why did Collins go from frightened to hero?
Why	Collins is a character to be pitied when he lets the mob of soldiers decide his actions. It seems as if his self-esteem is tied to the opinions of others until he assists the dying soldier, but the experience on the battlefield makes him a different person.

Step 4:

The student asks another related "why" question using a word or phrase from the most recent sentence.

    "Why" Question   Why does it matter that his self-esteem went up?

    Why of Why   From that moment on, Collins probably becomes a different person. It is doubtful if anyone would have been able to bully Collins into doing something he does not want to do.

Step 5:

The "why important" can offer an opportunity for the student to create some type of connection. This connection can be to other literature, history, or personal experience. In this case, the "why important" addresses a connection to human behavior.

    Why Important   The actions of Collins are important because they show how people can be pushed to behave in unexpected ways during difficult situations.

Step 6:

In the "as a result," the student describes the consequence and relates the sentences in the previous step.

    As a Result   As a result of doing the unexpected, Collins seems to see himself as a worthy, independent individual by the end of the story.

By writing these six parts continuously, the student has created an in-depth response that meets these criteria.

- The response is analytical.
- The response focuses on the reaction.
- The response explains why the reaction occurred.
- The response is organized.
- The response discusses the significance of the main idea.

Again, because of the response length the student actually produces two paragraphs. The first paragraph is comprised of steps one through three. The second paragraph is comprised of steps four through six.

The total rough draft response of the student looks like this.

Paragraph 1 (Steps 1, 2 and 3)

My first reaction is to pity Collins because he cares so much about what the other soldiers think. Collins has to risk his life in order to prove his worth to himself. However, my reaction of pity changes to respect by the middle of the story. It is doubtful if the men who bullied him to act would have had the courage to stop and assist the dying soldier in the middle of the battlefield. For example, Collins' first reaction to the dying man shows a frightened soldier who did not want to help. However, then, his actions are those of a hero who grants the dying man his final wish, even though Collins might lose his life. Initially, Collins is a character to be pitied when he lets the mob of soldiers decide his actions, but the experience on the battlefield makes him a different person.

Paragraph 2 (Steps 4, 5 and 6)

It seems as if his self-esteem is tied to the opinions of others until he assists the dying soldier. From that moment on, Collins probably becomes a different person. It is doubtful if anyone would have been able to bully Collins into doing something he does not want to do. The actions of Collins are important because they show how people can be pushed to behave in unexpected ways during difficult situations. As a result of doing the unexpected, Collins seems to see himself as a worthy, independent individual by the end of the story.

Situation 3: Analyzing Problem and Conflict

A student is asked to respond to this item.

Discuss one problem that is significant to the outcome of the story.

Step 1:

In the "main idea," the student describes the problem and briefly explains the problem.

Main Idea	One significant problem that Collins faces is whether or not to give dying man a drink of water. Even though the soldier is going to die with or without the water, Collins has to decide whether he is going to save his own life or do what he knows is the "right thing."

Step 2:

In the "for example," the student elaborates on the main idea with more detail. The teacher directs that this part contain, at least, one quote. When editing the response, the student might cross out the word "for example" in order to improve word flow. However, it is better to use this lead in phrase during the process of elaboration because the students stays more focused.

For Example	For example, at first, Collins yells, "I can't!" He keeps running to avoid the gunfire. The author writes: "He came running back to the wounded man." He returns to the soldier even though his eyes are filled with fear.

Step 3:

The student explains "why" this was/is a problem. The explanation needs to have some level of depth which shows the student understands the theme of the story.

"Why" Question	Why does Collins return?
Why	This is a problem for Collins because his first reaction tells him to keep going. His belief in doing the right thing takes over, regardless of the danger.

Step 4:

The student asks another "why" question using a word or phrase from the most recent sentence.

"Why" Question	Why does it matter that his moral beliefs took over?
Why of Why	By stopping for the dying man, Collins turns the foolish action of going after the water into a meaningful event. He changes from someone who

is acting stupidly into a hero. He stands up to a test of war and his helping the dying man changes the attitude of the soldiers toward him. Collins is no longer a clown in the eyes of the other men.

Step 5:

The "why important" requires the student to relate the problem to the theme and/or plot of the story.

Why Important   This problem is important to the theme and plot of the story because it sets the reader up for the ironic twist at the conclusion. Even though the other soldiers respect what Collins did, the two officers who fight over the bucket are not fazed. They do not care about Collins' bravery because they are so focused on themselves.

Step 6:

In the "as a result," the student specifies the consequence(s) of the "why important."

As a Result   As a result, the bucket lay on the ground "empty" after the two officers spilled the water. Nevertheless, the officers cannot eliminate how the "new" Collins feels about himself.

By writing the six parts continuously, the student has created an in-depth response that meets these criteria.

- The responses analytical.
- The response focuses on the problem.
- The response explains why the problem occurred.
- The response is organized.
- The response relates the problem to the theme and/or plot.

The total response of the student in rough draft looks like this.

Responses to steps 1, 2, and 3 plus the first sentence of the "why of why" become the first paragraph.

One significant problem that Collins faces is whether or not to give a dying man a drink of water. Even though the soldier is going to die with or without the water, Collins has to decide whether he is going to save his own life or do what he knows is the "right thing." For example, at first, Collins yells, "I can't!" He keeps running to avoid the gunfire. The author writes: "He came running back to the wounded man." He returns even though his eyes are filled with fear. This is a problem for Collins because his first reaction tells him to keep going. His belief in doing the right thing takes over. By stopping for the dying man, Collins turns the foolish action of going after the water into a meaningful event.

(Responses to steps four, five, and six become the second paragraph.)

Collins changes from someone who is acting stupidly into a hero. He stands up to a test of war and his helping the dying man changes the attitude of the soldiers toward him. Collins is no longer a clown in the eyes of the other men. This problem is important to the theme and plot of the story because it sets the reader up for the twist at the conclusion. Even though the other soldiers respect what Collins did, the two officers who fight over the bucket do not care. They do not care about Collins' bravery because they are so focused on themselves. As a result, the bucket lay on the ground "empty" after the two officers spill the water. Nevertheless, the officers cannot eliminate how the "new" Collins feels about himself.

Teachers can evaluate the six steps of the rough draft according to the rubric on the following page.

Structured Writing Rubric - English

Student			Teacher		Comment
Yes	No	The main idea is clear.	Yes	No	_____
Yes	No	The "for example" is complete, explaining one event or situation.	Yes	No	_____
Yes	No	The "why" explains the cause of the action discussed in the example.	Yes	No	_____
Yes	No	The first three parts of the paragraph are logical.	Yes	No	_____
Yes	No	The "why of why" provides additional insight.	Yes	No	_____
Yes	No	The "why important" clearly states the significance	Yes	No	_____
Yes	No	The action of the event is broken down.	Yes	No	_____
Yes	No	The "as a result" is a logical consequence that relates to the importance.	Yes	No	_____
Yes	No	The entire first draft paragraph is coherent.	Yes	No	_____
Yes	No	The student applies editing and revising skills.	Yes	No	_____

Student Comment: _____

_____

_____

Teacher Comment: _____

_____

_____

Applying the Structured Writing Process

ENGLISH

On the pages that follow are several different applications of the Structured Writing process tailored for English classes. Each sample contains the objective or purpose, and a description of the assignment in addition to each of the six steps.

There are two listings for each sample, one contains the student responses for each of the six steps, and the second contains the teacher notes for each step. Samples with teacher notes have the words "teacher notes" at the top of the page.

The following are samples for English classes:

Sample 1:   Persuasive response

Sample 2:   Expository analysis

Sample 3:   Analysis of a poem or song

Sample 4:   Personal narrative

Sample 5:   Analysis in a letter

ENGLISH - Sample 1   Persuasive Response

Purpose

A CHARACTER PERSUADING ANOTHER CHARACTER
To justify actions or behavior to someone or a group that disagrees.

Assignment – This is part of a persuasive response from English class.

Brutus writes a letter to the Roman people on his deathbed to justify his actions.

- The student presents the beliefs and attitudes of the character.
- The student uses events from the text to support the position.
- The student takes a realistic perspective given the character's personality.

Step 1: Main Idea

The people of Rome have judged me harshly because they have concluded that I have behaved selfishly. My motives for assassinating Julius Caesar are noble; my love for Caesar does not compare with my love for Rome.

Step 2: For Example

For example, Caesar's accomplishments were many. His military victories, such as against Egypt, and his reforms, such as those that provided food for the poor, made Rome great. Yet, while we all cheer for these accomplishments, Caesar's desire to make himself dictator for life smothers the purpose of our republic.

Step 3: Why

Caesar possessed this desire because he began to see himself as Rome, not as a servant of Rome. Over time, his decisions would prevent the Senate from having any real power at all.

Step 4: Why of Why

The Senate would continue to lose power because Caesar's real ambition was to make himself the king of Rome.

Step 5: Why Important

Your judgment is important to me because my decision to assassinate Caesar was based on the reality that he was going to destroy our Roman way of life.

Step 6: As a Result

As a result, the people of Rome must remember the words I have previously stated. "If then that friend demand why Brutus rose against Caesar, this is my answer—not that I loved Caesar less, but that I loved Rome more." (Act 3, Scene 2)

ENGLISH - Sample 1 (TEACHER'S NOTES)	Persuasive Response

Purpose

A CHARACTER PERSUADING ANOTHER CHARACTER
To justify actions or behavior to someone or a group that disagrees.

Assignment – This is part of a persuasive response from English class.

Brutus writes a letter on his deathbed to the Roman people to justify his actions.

- The student adopts a tone that reminds the reader of Brutus.
- The student uses historical events to convince the reader.
- The student understands the audience being addressed.

Step 1: Main Idea

This main idea sets the tone for the rest of the response. The initial sentence is strong with the word "harshly." The second sentence is based on the words of Brutus spoken in the play.

Step 2: For Example

The details in the first part of this segment show the writer does not understand the greatness of Caesar, as did Brutus. The argument becomes powerful with the word "yet" that alerts the reader to Caesar's motives.

Step 3: Why

The "why" is comprised of basic inferences that the student should understand from reading the play. The people need to hear an answer to the questions: Why do his motives exist and why do they matter?

Step 4: Why of Why

This section plays upon the Senate losing power because the writer needs to convince the people that this action is not in their best interests.

Step 5: Why Important

The word "judgment" goes back to the main idea. The student describes why the opening two sentences mean so much. If the persuasion works, the reader will shake his/her head "yes" at this point.

Step 6: As a Result

The student closes with a quote from Brutus that is the basis of the main idea in statement one. The type of the persuasion is circular in nature. The main idea is repeated as the consequence at the end of this part of the argument. This technique only works in certain persuasive responses.

ENGLISH - Sample 2   Expository Analysis

Purpose

PRESENTING A PROBLEM THAT IS SIGNIFICANT
To develop a basic analysis of how the problem affects a character.

Assignment – This is an expository analysis after discussing a short story.

The student selects a problem that affects the main character from "A Mystery of Heroism" by Stephen Crane.

- The students have determined that the story has multiple problems.
- The student selects a problem that has an impact on the character's life.
- The student includes relevant events and logically analyzes the events.

Step 1: Main Idea

One significant problem that Collins faces is whether or not to give the dying man a drink of water. Even though the soldier is going to die with or without water, Collins has to decide if he's going to save his own life or do what he knows is the "right thing."

Step 2: For Example

For example, at first Collins yells, "I can't!" He keeps running to avoid the gunfire. The author writes: "He came back running to the wounded man." Collins returns even though his eyes were "filled with terror."

Step 3: Why

This is a problem for Collins because his first reaction tells him to keep going. His moral beliefs have to take over for his instincts.

Step 4: Why of Why

By stopping for the dying man, Collins turns the foolish action of going after the water into a meaningful event. It changes from someone who is acting stupidly into a hero.

Step 5: Why Important

This problem is important to the theme and plot of the story because the other soldiers began to view Collins as a hero and not as a "clown." Ironically, the two officers who fight over the bucket of water at the end of the story do not care about Collins' bravery.

Step 6: As a Result

As a result, these officers became the real clowns, while Collins can feel positive about his compassion.

ENGLISH - Sample 2 (TEACHER'S NOTES)	Expository Analysis

Purpose

PRESENTING A PROBLEM THAT IS SIGNIFICANT
To develop a basic analysis of how the problem affects a character.

Assignment – This is an expository analysis after discussing a short story.

The student selects a problem that affects the main character from "A Mystery of Heroism" by Stephen Crane.

- The student explains the problem clearly.
- The student selects a problem that has an impact on the character's life.
- The student includes relevant events and logically analyzes the events.

Step 1: Main Idea

The main idea sets up the dilemma that Collins faces. What will his conscience tell him to do? The main idea is lengthy because there needs to be an in-depth exploration of this question.

Step 2: For Example

This example catches the essence of the dilemma. The student uses the author's language to clarify the two parts of the example. The author's words are interspersed with his/her own commentary.

Step 3: Why

This "why" is an important inference; the word "instinct" represents the inside of the writer.

Step 4: Why of Why

This segment asks: Why did the instinct matter? The choice Collins made changed his life. He inevitably would look at himself differently. The writer also discusses how men would view him, but perhaps Collins does not care about the men's perceptions anymore.

Step 5: Why Important

The writer specifies why the problem is important to the main character, but also its significance to the men and the two officers. The writer wants the reader to know that the officers switch places with Collins.

Step 6: As a Result

This "as a result" presents the impact of the problem on the main character.

ENGLISH - Sample 3	Relating a Poem to a Song

Purpose

RELATING TEXT TO TEXT
To determine similarities/differences between the messages of texts.

Assignment – This is relating a poem to a song.

The poem is "I, Too, Am America" and the song is "The Death of Emmett Till."

- The student reads and discusses the poem and, then, the song.
- The student discusses the central message(s) of both texts.
- The student creates a logical connection between the two sources.

Step 1: Main Idea

Langston Hughes centers on the idea that even though racism has happened in America for generations, it will not stop him from achieving. Bob Dylan's lyrics are about a boy being a victim of racism that kept him from achieving.

Step 2: For Example

For example, Hughes makes it clear that racist forces are not going to keep him down when he writes: "But I laugh/And grow strong. Tomorrow/I'll be at the table/When company comes." Dylan makes it clear that the same forces that Hughes will hurdle have destroyed Emmett Till. Dylan writes: "This song is just a reminder to remind your fellow man/That this kind of thing still lives today in that ghost-robed Ku Klux Klan."

Step 3: Why

Hughes states his message because he wants to tell African Americans not to let the past put them down. Dylan states these lyrics because he wants to get across the message that the evils of racism are not dead enough and that the past still exists.

Step 4: Why of Why

Hughes sees a time when African Americans are going to take their place as the powerful and wealthy. Those were used to being in power are going to realize that African Americans are strong. Dylan's statement about racism is to show that the Emmett Till tragedy could happen today.

Step 5: Why Important

Both messages are important because they are two sides of the same story. Hughes is only too aware of the powers of racism, but he is showing a positive reaction. Dylan is showing the other side of the same story; Emmett Till was a victim, and people need to be reminded.

Step 6: As a Result

As a result, the individual who lives racism, Hughes, is optimistic, while the person commenting on racism is pessimistic.

ENGLISH - Sample 3 (TEACHER'S NOTES)	Relating a Poem to a Song

Purpose

RELATING TEXT TO TEXT
To determine similarities/differences between the messages of texts.

Assignment – This is relating a poem to a song.

The poem is "I, Too, Am America" and the song is "The Death of Emmett Till."

- The student understands the inferences of both artists.
- The student applies the evaluative message of both artists.
- The student compares the messages of both artists.

Step 1: Main Idea

The main idea is broken into two sentences, establishing the comparison. The writer could have combined the content of both statements into one sentence. However, the striking difference between the intent of both authors would not have been as evident.

Step 2: For Example

The words of Hughes and Dylan reinforced the message in the main idea. The writer has chosen quotes that demonstrate literal support for the main idea.

Step 3: Why

The "why" component asks: Why does each artist write the words that are part of the poem or song? The writer briefly discusses the reasons and highlights the different sets of emotions. Hughes seems determined and Dylan hopes to be a messenger telling people the past is not over.

Step 4: Why of Why

This segment focuses on following: Why does each artist care about this message? The writer draws this comparison clearly by stating Hughes' goal in contrast to Dylan's warning.

Step 5: Why Important

The statement of importance centers on the insight that both individuals would agree with each other's message. The writer discusses the idea of "two sides of the same coin"; this refers to the notion that similar circumstances can create two very different situations.

Step 6: As a Result

The writer mentions the irony that Hughes who experienced the racism is optimistic, while Dylan who did not is pessimistic. This insight draws an interesting contrast.

ENGLISH - Sample 4	**Personal Narrative**

Purpose

TAKING THE POINT OF VIEW OF A CHARACTER
To evaluate why a character behaves in a certain manner.
To take a specific point of view.

Assignment – This is a personal narrative paragraph based on the student assuming the role of a character.

The writer takes the role of Athena after reading "The Myth of Arachne."

- The student describes personal thoughts and feelings.
- The student shows an appreciation for events and behaviors.
- The student attempts to show the cause(s) for behavior(s).

Step 1: Main Idea

Arachne is a very arrogant lady who does not show proper respect.

Step 2: For Example

For example, she mocked me when I posed as the old woman, making it clear that she was the most talented weaver. Even when she realized that I was disguised as the old lady, she failed to apologize.

Step 3: Why

She mocked the old woman because she is unable to show respect for anyone, let alone a goddess. She could not apologize because she cannot appreciate the role of the gods and their power.

Step 4: Why of Why

Arachne's lack of respect exists because the people around her have reinforced her hubristic beliefs. If she had begged for forgiveness immediately after realizing that I was the old woman, I would not have changed her into the spider.

Step 5: Why Important

Arachne's arrogance is important to remember because other mortals might be tempted to behave in a similar way. These humans need to think twice and recall Arachne's fate.

Step 6: As a Result

As a result of Arachne's fate, she will spend eternity in a prison of hopelessness.

ENGLISH - Sample 4 (TEACHER'S NOTES)	**Personal Narrative**

Purpose

TAKING THE POINT OF VIEW OF A CHARACTER
To evaluate why a character behaves in a certain manner.
To take a specific point of view.

Assignment – This is a personal narrative paragraph based on the student assuming the role of a character.

The writer takes the role of Athena after reading "The Myth of Arachne."

- The student relates the underlying reason with text.
- The student produces a voice that fits the character.
- The student relates evaluative comments to events.

Step 1: Main Idea

Athena, the goddess, showing her outrage through the main idea statement. The writer adopts her voice as someone who is astounded at Arachne's attitude.

Step 2: For Example

The example illustrates Athena disbelief on two levels. First she would be so disrespectful to an old lady and, second, she would not realize her error and try to make amends.

Step 3: Why

The writer establishes a one-to-one correspondence between each sentence in the example and this segment. Why does she fail to show this respect?

Step 4: Why of Why

In this section, the writer uses his/her inferential understanding of the myth to create a logical part of the response. Athena does not actually state these ideas in the text, but it is fair to say that she could have stated them.

Step 5: Why Important

The writer creates a lesson for all mortals to keep in mind. Arachne's experience is important because others must learn from it or suffer the same fate.

Step 6: As a Result

This statement tells about the literal fate of the character. Arachne's consequence will be to spend the rest of her life in misery.

ENGLISH - Sample 5	**Paragraph From a Letter**

Purpose

A CHARACTER DESCRIBING HIS/HER POSITION
To discuss the underlying issue that affects behavior.

Assignment – This is a paragraph from a letter about why the character behaved in a certain way.

Letter from Beneatha, the daughter, in A Raisin in the Sun by Lorraine Hansberry to her mama.

- The letter demonstrates an understanding of events.
- The student takes a point of view that is logical to events and actions.
- The student shows an understanding of circumstances that caused events.

Step 1: Main Idea

I am an independent person who is proud of my African heritage, and who believes that African Americans must learn from this heritage.

Step 2: For Example

For example, I am excited to wear the native clothing from Nigeria given to me by Asagai. I cannot believe that Ruth, my sister-in-law, makes fun of this clothing. I, also, am proud to show my hair cut like my sisters in Nigeria.

Step 3: Why

I am tired of black people giving in to the demands of the white people. Some might say that my beliefs are radical, but so be it. I want to learn more about my heritage, and I want my family to respect me for it.

Step 4: Why of Why

African Americans need to learn about their routes because they must do more than assimilate into white society.

Step 5: Why Important

The idea of being independent is important because I refuse to listen to the narrow view of my brother, and I resent the limited view of George. We, as a people, will never get ahead if African Americans listen to the Walters and Georges of this world.

Step 6: As a Result

As a result of celebrating this independence, African Americans will not be threatened by white people who expect us to assimilate.

ENGLISH - Sample 5 (TEACHER'S NOTES)	Paragraph From a Letter

Purpose

A CHARACTER DESCRIBING HIS/HER POSITION
To discuss the underlying issue that affects behavior.

Assignment – This is a paragraph from a letter about why the character behaved in a certain way.

Letter from Beneatha, the daughter, in A Raisin in the Sun by Lorraine Hansberry to her mama.

- The student uses text to justify the actions of the character.
- The student uses the voice of the character to present a valid viewpoint.
- The student embeds the "big picture" into the paragraph.

Step 1: Main Idea

This statement represents an inference that Beneatha easily could have proclaimed. The statement becomes the main theme of her commentary in the letter.

Step 2: For Example

The writer makes a point of emphasizing Beneatha's preference of clothing and hairstyle. In addition, the writer uses Ruth's attitude as an example of those who do not value their African heritage.

Step 3: Why

This component expresses "why" Beneatha feels so strongly about identifying with her roots. The words "I am tired . . . " show that her patience is thin.

Step 4: Why of Why

The writer asks: Why is her patient so thin? The majority of Americans expect Beneatha to assimilate into the "white society." The key word is "assimilate." Beneatha detests the idea of assimilating.

Step 5: Why Important

The writer makes the connection between Walter and George to the idea of assimilation. This segment of the response is an inference based on the ongoing responses of Walter and George.

Step 6: As a Result

This consequence is ironic because the white people are intimidating African Americans who are moving into certain neighborhoods.

Part 2

Structuring a Response to a Science Text, Article or Experiment

Students often are responsible for reading a section of text or an article about a particular topic and responding to the content in one or more paragraphs. Or, students are responsible for write a paragraph discussing a conclusion from an experiment. Students can use the six steps for paragraph writing when responding to a question or prompt about the reading.

The implementation of the six-step process is especially beneficial for students who have comprehension difficulties. When students respond to each of the six steps of the Structured Writing process, they are building literal, synthesis, inferential, evaluative and application comprehension.

The idea of reading an article, recalling significant information, and writing a paragraph containing analysis can be very difficult for students who are not highly proficient. Consequently, students in this group need a system that will allow them to grasp onto meaningful information immediately and connect that information so that their written paragraphs are accurate, insightful and coherent.

The Structured Writing process, also, is extremely beneficial when students are expected to read articles about a controversial issue and to write an explanation discussing their understanding of the topic. The six-step writing process becomes an organized way for students to think about the content and to present their point of view. In essence, the sequence of paragraph writing steps serves a double purpose. First, students are recording annotated notes in an organized manner. Second, students are placing these annotated notes into meaningful paragraphs. Therefore, students use the process for recording information and writing analytically.

The explanations in this section demonstrate both of these purposes. Based on the article, students record responses to each of the six steps of the process. These responses become the basis for an in-depth analytical paragraph. Proficiency with this process does require a great deal of practice. However, this practice can become part of the curriculum. Teachers can select articles that complement concepts already presented during class or sections of texts that merit a great deal of analysis. Consequently, practice increases the comprehension of important concepts on which the students need to be assessed, as well as producing meaningful paragraphs.

The students follow the prescribed six steps for the Structured Paragraph.

    Step 1: main idea or stated reason
    Step 2: for example
    Step 3: why
    Step 4: why of why
    Step 5: why important
    Step 6: as a result

Teachers can blend this paragraph writing process into directed instruction. The connection from instruction to discussion to writing brings about heighted understanding. Here is one simple way to achieve this result.

Step 1: The teacher and class discuss the main purpose of the learning experience then, each student records the purpose in an in-depth statement.

Step 2: The teacher and class discuss details and data related to the main purpose then, students record two or three pieces of relevant supporting information.

Step 3 and **Step 4:** The students work in pairs to discuss "why" the details support the main idea. Then, each student records his or her response.

Step 5: The teacher and students discuss why the purpose, details and data are important to the topic. Then the students record their response.

Step 6: The students work in pairs to determine logical consequences related to their explanations in steps 1 through 5. Then each student records his or her response in one or two sentences.

This comprehension building is completed during the class period. Consequently students leave class with an in-depth paragraph representing their thinking about the content.

Situation 1: Analyzing Experimental Conclusion[*]

In a high school biology class, students conducted a lab to determine how light intensity affects the rate of photosynthesis on the water plant elodea. Students were able to measure the rate of photosynthesis by counting the number of bubbles produced at varying distances of light.

Two beakers were filled with water and a sprig of water plant was placed into each beaker and then covered with a test tube. Students placed one beaker in the shade and the other beaker beside a lamp.

The students, then, systematically changed the distance of the beaker from the lamp. (Distance from source: 5 cm, 10 cm, 15 cm, 20 cm, 25 cm and 30 cm.) They counted the bubbles given off by each sprig of the water plant.

The teacher wants students to write a paragraph discussing a significant conclusion drawn from the photosynthesis lab. Here is a sample conclusion using the six steps of the Structured Writing process.

Step 1:

In the "main idea," the student describes one key conclusion drawn from the experiment. The student records the conclusion in one in-depth sentence. This sentence needs to contain specific terminology.

Main Idea   Based on the experiment, the water plants produce more bubbles of oxygen gas when placed next to the light source and fewer bubbles as the beaker was moved further away from the light.

Step 2:

In the "for example," the student cites data recorded during the experiment to support the conclusion. When placing the six responses into a paragraph, the student might cross out the words "for example" in order to improve word flow. However, it is better to lead with this phrase during the first draft process because the student stays more focused.

For Example   For example, when the beaker was placed 5 cm from the light source, the plant produced a total of 55 bubbles per minute. However, when the beaker was placed 30 cm from the light source, the plants only produced 4 bubbles per minute. No bubbles were produced by the plant place completely in the shade.

[*]Responses to Situation 1 were completed in collaboration with Steven Anderson, biology teacher at Ridgefield High School in Connecticut.

Step 3:

The student explains "why" this happened. In addition, the student states "why" the light affected the experimental results. The explanation needs to have some level of depth which shows the student understands the central concepts. The student poses a simple "why" question to aid in completing this part of the writing and thinking process.

"Why" Question	Why did the light source cause this to happen?
Why	This happened because all photoautotrophs, including plants, required sunlight to carry out photosynthesis. Pigments located within the leaves of plants can absorb more light when placed closer to a light source; this increased the overall rate of photosynthesis.

Step 4:

The student poses another "why" question to aid in completing this part of the writing and thinking process. The student picks a phrase from the third step to use as an anchor in a question for this part of the process. The student chooses the phrase "overall rate" to be incorporated in question. This step in science requires the inclusion of relevant terminology.

Why of Why Question	Why did this increase the overall rate?
Why of Why	Photosynthesis is a process that harnesses the energy found in sunlight and converts it into chemical energy that the plant can use. During this process, oxygen gas is also released as a by-product of photosynthesis. Therefore, more bottles of oxygen gas will be produced during higher rates of photosynthesis.

Step 5:

The "why important" requires the student to tell the significance of the conclusion. In this case, the student centers on the significance of light energy which is the main idea in step one.

Why Important	Plants can only survive if they are able to absorb a sufficient amount of light. Plants exposed to prolonged periods of darkness will not be able to photosynthesize. Without light energy, plants cannot produce the sugars they need to provide the chemical energy.

Step 6:

In the "as a result," the student states the consequence or consequences. The student relates the response to the step to the previous sentences.

As a Result   As a result, plants placed in areas of low light intensity will not survive due to low levels of glucose necessary for cellular work. However, plants placed in areas with medium to high light intensity will do well because of a higher rate of photosynthesis.

By writing these six parts continuously, the student has created an in-depth response that meets these criteria.

- The responses analytical.
- The response focuses on the conclusion.
- The response explains the relation of the conclusion to the data and information.
- The response is organized.
- The response makes a valid connection.

☞   **Keep this in mind:** This analytical conclusion can become a section of the student's lab report.

The student's analytical responses to the article become the basis for one or two paragraphs. Here are the six responses of the Structured Writing Paragraph.

Step 1   Based on the experiment, the water plants produced more bubbles of oxygen gas were placed next to the light source and fewer bubbles as the beaker was moved further away from the light.

Step 2   For example, when the beaker was placed 5 cm from the light source, the plant produced a total of 55 bubbles per minute. However, when the beaker was placed 30 cm from the light source, the plants only produced 4 bubbles per minute. No bubbles were produced by the plant place completely in the shade.

Step 3   This happened because all photoautotrophs, including plants, require sunlight to carry out photosynthesis. Pigments located within the leaves of plants can absorb more light when placed closer to a light source; this increased the overall rate of photosynthesis.

Step 4   Photosynthesis is the process that harnesses the energy found in sunlight and converts it into chemical energy that the plant can use. During this process, oxygen gas is also released as a by-product of photosynthesis. Therefore, more bubbles of oxygen gas will be produced during higher rates of photosynthesis.

Step 5   Plants can only survive if they are able to absorb a sufficient amount of light. Plants exposed to prolonged periods of darkness will not be able to photosynthesize. Without light energy, plants cannot produce the sugars they need that provide the chemical energy.

Step 6   As a result, plants placed in areas of low light intensity will not survive due to low levels of glucose necessary for cellular work. However, plants placed in areas with medium to high light intensity will do well because of a higher rate of photosynthesis.

Because of the length, the student can break the six responses into two rough draft paragraphs. Steps one, two and three become one paragraph; the remaining three steps form a second paragraph of the response.

The paragraphs should reveal that the student possesses an understanding of key concepts at these comprehension levels: literal, synthesis, and inferential. These paragraphs can comprise the "conclusion" section of the lab report. Here are the two paragraphs discussing the conclusion drawn from the photosynthesis lab.

Paragraph 1 (steps 1, 2, and 3)

Based on the experiment, the water plants produced more bubbles of oxygen gas when placed next to the light source and fewer bubbles as the beaker was moved further away from the light. For example, when the beaker was placed 5 cm from the light source, the plant produced a total of 55 bubbles per minute. However, when the beaker was placed 30 cm from the light source, the plant only produced 4 bubbles per minute. No bubbles were produced by the plant placed completely in the shade. This happened because all photoautotrophs, including plants, require sunlight to carry out photosynthesis. Pigments located within the leaves of plants can absorb more light when placed closer to a light source; this increased the overall rate of photosynthesis.

Paragraph 2 (steps 4, 5, and 6)

Photosynthesis is a process that harnesses the energy found in sunlight and converts it into chemical energy that the plant can use. During this process, oxygen gas is also released as a by-product of photosynthesis. Therefore, more bubbles of oxygen gas will be produced during higher rates of photosynthesis.

Plants can only survive if they are able to absorb a sufficient amount of light. Plants exposed to prolonged periods of darkness will not be able to photosynthesize. Without light energy, plants cannot produce the sugars they need that provide the chemical energy. As a result, plants placed in areas of low light intensity will not survive due to low levels of glucose necessary for cellular work. However, plants placed in areas with medium to high light intensity will do well because of a higher rate of photosynthesis.

Situation 2: Understanding a Point of View

The students of a ninth grade science class have been learning about the topic of *hormones*. The teacher has given the students an article that focuses on *injecting hormones into dairy cows to increase milk production*. The teacher has assigned the article because she wants students to understand the concept that science has economic and health ramifications.

The teacher has spent class time reading and discussing the article.[*] After the discussion, the teacher asks the students to apply the six-step Structured Writing process. The students already understand the process. The students are not allowed to use the article when recording their initial responses to the steps in the structure, except when locating an appropriate quotation. The teacher wants to improve student ability to recall vital information; therefore, she builds student recall into the lesson. Once the students have provided their initial responses to each of the six steps, they can refer back to the article for additional information; however, the students are not allowed to copy from the article, except when including a quotation.

The students are required to write their paragraph from either the point of view of the farmers or the boycotters. The teacher has each student select a paper from a hat identifying on which point of view the response focuses.

Here's one example of a student's set of responses. This student has picked a slip of paper saying "boycotters."

Step 1:

In the "main idea," the student describes one key idea or problem presented in the content. With this "main idea," the student is citing the central issue being described in the article. The student could write about this issue in one sentence; however, the student realizes that it is clearer to state the issue in two sentences. Therefore, the main idea in this instance is actually two sentences.

Main Idea   Many farmers are injecting hormones into their herd of dairy cattle to increase the amount of milk produced. However, groups of protesters have organized boycotts to call people's attention to the problem.

Step 2:

In the "for example," the student uses a quotation to elaborate on the main idea. When placing the six responses into a paragraph, the student might cross out the words "for example" in order to improve word flow. However, it is better to lead with this phrase during the process because the student stays more focused.

---

[*] Josie Glausiusz, "Flap Over Milk", *Discovery Magazine*, January 1995.

For Example   For example, Ronnie Cummins, a boycott leader, states the protesters point of view. "The public has the right to know whether food has been genetically engineered or not."

Step 3:

The student explains "why" this person stated these words. In addition, the student states "why" the farmers want to practice genetic engineering. The explanation needs have some level of depth which shows the student understands the central concepts of the article. The student poses a simple "why" question to aid in completing this part of the writing and thinking process.

"Why" Question   Why does Cummins believe people have a right to know?

Why   Mr. Cummins wants to emphasize that the hormones injected into the dairy cows are passed along to the humans who drink the milk. He believes that the dairy farmers care more about profits that about the health of the people who drink the milk, especially babies.

Step 4:

The students pose another "why" question to aid in completing this part of the writing and thinking process. The students pick a phrase from the third step to use as an anchor in the question for this part of the process. The students chooses the phrase "the health of the people" to be incorporated in the question.

Why of Why Question   Why is the health of the people part of this?

Why of Why   Farmers care so much about profits that they are injecting the cows with antibiotics to cure infections from the hormone injections. The farmers are not concerned that these antibiotics are being passed on to consumers to the food chain.

Step 5:

The "why important" requires the student to tell the significance of the problem. In this case, the student centers on the significance of those boycotting because that is the emphasis of the responses.

Why Important   Cummins believes that this problem is significant because humans might become resistant to certain antibiotics as they move from the milk into human bodies. The dairy farmers want to stop the boycott because they are afraid that public awareness will cause people to stop buying milk.

Step 6:

In the "as a result," the student states the consequence or consequences. The student relates the response to the step to the previous sentences.

As a Result	As a result, many dairy farmers remain frustrated because the world market for milk has increased and the farmers have to find ways to increase production. However, the boycotters want to educate the public about the possible danger of these injections.

By writing these six parts continuously, the student has created an in-depth response that meets these criteria.

- The responses analytical.
- The response focuses on the quotation.
- The response explains the relation of the quotation to the theme of the work.
- The response is organized.
- The response makes a valid connection.

☞   **Keep this in mind:** Students can develop their Structured Writing paragraphs as a foundation for heightened comprehension of a complex issue. In this instance, students can create analytical paragraphs representing each point of view.

The student's analytical responses to the article become the basis for one or two paragraphs. Here are the six responses of the Structured Writing paragraph.

Step 1	Many farmers are injecting hormones into their herd of dairy cattle to increase the amount of milk produced. However, groups of protesters have organized boycotts to call people's attention to the problem.
Step 2	For example, Ronnie Cummins, a boycott leader, states that the protesters point of view. "The public has the right to know whether food has been genetically engineered or not."
Step 3	Mr. Cummins wants to emphasize that the hormones injected into the dairy cows are passed along to humans who drink the milk. He believes that the dairy farmers care more about profits than about the health of the people who drink the milk, especially babies.

Step 4   Farmers care so much about profits that they are injecting the cows with antibiotics to cure the infections from the hormone injections. The farmers are not concerned that these antibiotics are being passed on to consumers through the food chain.

Step 5   Cummins believes that this problem is significant because humans might become resistant to certain antibiotics as they move from the milk into their bodies. The dairy farmers want to stop the boycott because they are afraid that public awareness will cause people to stop buying milk.

Step 6   As a result, many dairy farmers remain frustrated because the world market for milk has increased, and the farmers have to find ways to increase production. However, the boycotters want to educate the public about the possible danger of these injections.

Because of the length, the student can break the six responses into two rough draft paragraphs. Steps one, two and three become one paragraph; the remaining three steps form a second paragraph of the response.

Students can present these analytical paragraphs as if they are attempting to persuade an audience to adopt their point of view. The paragraphs should reveal that the student possesses an understanding of the article at these comprehension levels: literal, synthesis, and inferential.

Paragraph 1 (steps 1, 2, and 3)

Many farmers are injecting hormones into their herd of dairy cattle to increase the amount of milk produced. However, groups of protesters have organized boycotts to call people's attention to the problem. For example, Ronnie Cummins, a boycott leader, states the protester's point of view. "The public has the right to know whether food has been genetically engineered or not." Mr. Cummins wants to emphasize that the hormones injected into the dairy cows are passed along to humans who drink the milk. He believes that the dairy farmers care more about profits than about the health of the people who drink the milk, especially babies.

Paragraph 2 (steps 4, 5, and 6)

Farmers care so much about profits that they are injecting the cows with antibiotics to cure the infections from the hormone injections. The farmers are not concerned that these antibiotics are being passed onto consumers through the food chain. Cummins believes that this problem is significant because humans might become resistant to certain antibiotics as they move from the milk into their bodies. The dairy farmers want to stop the boycott because they are afraid that public awareness will cause people to stop buying milk. As a result, many dairy farmers remain frustrated because the world market for milk has increased and the farmers have to find ways to increase production. However, the boycotters want to educate the public about the possible danger of these injections.

Situation 3: Analyzing Data[*]

In a middle school science class, the students have conducted a lab related to heart rate. Students conducted the experiment to determine the effects of varying amounts of physical activity on their heart rate. Students began by checking their own heart rate prior to any form of physical activity; this was done by measuring the number of heartbeats per minute.

Once students recorded their resting heart rate (RHR), they proceeded to perform a variety of physical activities. This included the following: jogging in place for 30 seconds, then taking heart rate; jogging in place for 1 minute, then taking heart rate; finally, jogging in place for 2 minutes and recording heart rate.

The teacher uses the six steps of Structured Writing for students to record a paragraph analyzing data for a section of their lab reports. Here is a sample conclusion using the six steps of the Structured Writing process.

Step 1:

In the "main idea," the student describes one key conclusion drawn from the experiment. The student records the conclusion in one in-depth sentence. This sentence needs to contain specific terminology.

Main Idea	Based on the experiment, a person's heart rate increases as he or she performs longer periods of physical activity.

Step 2:

In the "for example," the student cites data recorded during the experiment to support the conclusion.

For Example	For example, my resting heart rate with no physical activity was found to be 70 beats per minute. However, my heart rate increased to 105 beats per minute after 30 seconds of exercise and to 135 beats per minute after 2 minutes of heavy exercise.

Step 3:

The student explains "why" this happened. The explanation needs have some level of depth which shows the student understands the central concepts of the experiment. The student poses a simple "why" question to aid in completing this part of the writing and thinking process.

[*]Responses to Situation 3 were completed in collaboration with Steven Anderson, biology teacher at Ridgefield High School in Connecticut.

"Why" Question   Why does did exercise make a difference?

Why   This happened because as physical activity increases, muscle cells consume more oxygen. When there are low levels of oxygen in your blood, the heart must be faster to deliver more oxygen rich blood to the rest of your muscle cells.

Step 4:

The student poses another "why" question to aid in completing this part of the writing and thinking process. The student picks a phrase from the third step to use as an anchor in the question for this part of the process. The student chooses the word "oxygen" to be incorporated in question. This step in science requires the inclusion of relevant terminology.

Why of Why Question   Why does the amount of oxygen matter?

Why of Why   Our body uses oxygen to help break down sugars to release energy for your cells. Without this oxygen, your cells are unable to make energy for your body, and you are unable to continue the physical activity. Deeper breathing brings in more oxygen to the lungs and eventually to the heart. The oxygen can then be delivered to the rest of the body.

Step 5:

The "why important" requires the student to tell the significance of the conclusion. In this case, the student centers on the significance of the body needing energy.

Why Important   Our body needs a constant supply of energy in order to survive, in this case to keep exercising. However, without an adequate supply of sugars and oxygen in the bloodstream, the body begins to slow down and will eventually stop.

Step 6:

In the "as a result," the student states the consequence or consequences. The student relates the response to the step to the previous sentences.

As a Result   As a result, heart rate must increase as levels of activity increase. This will bring a fresh supply of oxygen to the cells, allowing them to generate more energy and helping them to continue daily activity.

By writing these six parts continuously, the student has created an in-depth response that meets these criteria.

- The responses analytical.
- The response focuses on the conclusion.
- The response explains the relation of the conclusion to the data.
- The response is organized.
- The response applies information to the real world.

The student's analytical responses become the rough draft for the conclusion. Here are the six responses of the Structured Writing process.

Step 1   Based on the experiment, a person's heart rate increases as he or she performs longer periods of physical activity.

Step 2   For example, my resting heart rate with no physical activity was found to be 70 beats per minute. However, my heart rate increased to 105 beats per minute after 30 seconds of exercise and to 135 beats per minute after 2 minutes of heavy exercise.

Step 3   This happened because as physical activity increases, muscle cells consume more oxygen. When there are low levels of oxygen in your blood, the heart must beat faster to deliver more oxygen rich blood to the rest of your muscle cells.

Step 4   Our body uses oxygen to help break down sugars to release energy for your cells. Without this oxygen, your cells are unable to make energy for your body, and you are unable to continue the physical activity. Deeper breathing brings in more oxygen into the lungs and eventually to the heart. The oxygen can then be delivered to the rest of the body.

Step 5   Our body needs a constant supply of energy in order to survive, in this case to keep exercising. However, without enough of a supply of sugars and oxygen in the bloodstream, the body begins to slow down and will eventually stop.

Step 6   As a result, heart rate must increase as levels of activity increase. This will bring a fresh supply of oxygen to the cells, allowing them to generate more energy and helping to continued daily activity.

Because of the length, the student breaks the six responses into two rough draft paragraphs. Steps one, two and three become one paragraph; the remaining three steps form a second paragraph of the response.

The paragraphs should reveal that the student possesses an understanding of the content at these comprehension levels: literal, synthesis, and inferential.

Two paragraphs discussing the conclusion drawn from the heart rate experiment.

Paragraph one (steps 1, 2, and 3)

> Based on the experiment, a person's heart rate increases as he or she performs longer periods of physical activity. For example, my resting heart rate with no physical activity was found to be 70 beats per minute. However, my heart rate increased to 105 beats per minute after 30 seconds of exercise and to 135 beats per minute after 2 minutes of heavy exercise. This happened because as physical activity increases, muscle cells consume more oxygen. When there are low levels of oxygen in your blood, the heart must beat faster to deliver more oxygen rich blood to the rest of your muscle cells.

Paragraph two (steps 4, 5, and 6)

> Our body uses oxygen to help break down sugars to release energy for your cells. Without this oxygen, your cells are unable to make energy for your body, and you are unable to continue the physical activity. Deeper breathing brings in more oxygen to the lungs and eventually to the heart. The oxygen can then be delivered to the rest of the body. Our body needs a constant supply of energy in order to survive, in this case to keep exercising. However, without enough of a supply of sugars and oxygen in the bloodstream, the body begins to slow down and will eventually stop. As a result, heart rate must increase as levels of activity increase. This will bring a fresh supply of oxygen to the cells, allowing them to generate more energy and helping to continue daily activity.

Teachers can evaluate the six steps of the rough draft according to the rubric on the following page.

Structured Writing Rubric - Science

Student			Teacher		Comment
Yes	No	The main idea is clear.	Yes	No	_____
Yes	No	The "for example" is complete, explaining one event or situation.	Yes	No	_____
Yes	No	The "why" explains the cause of the action discussed in the example.	Yes	No	_____
Yes	No	The first three parts of the paragraph are logical.	Yes	No	_____
Yes	No	The "why of why" provides additional insight.	Yes	No	_____
Yes	No	The "why important" clearly states the significance	Yes	No	_____
Yes	No	The meaning of the information is broken down.	Yes	No	_____
Yes	No	The "as a result" is a logical consequence that relates to the importance.	Yes	No	_____
Yes	No	The entire first draft paragraph is coherent.	Yes	No	_____
Yes	No	The student applies editing and revising skills.	Yes	No	_____

Student Comment: _____

_____

_____

Teacher Comment: _____

_____

_____

Applying the Structured Writing Process

SCIENCE

On the pages that follow are several different applications of the Structured Writing process tailored for science classes. Each sample contains the objective or purpose, and a description of the assignment in addition to each of the six steps.

There are two listings for each sample, one contains the student responses for each of the six steps and the second contains the teacher notes for each step. Samples with teacher notes have the words "teacher notes" at the top of the page.

The following are the samples for Science class.

Sample 1:   Persuasive response

Sample 2:   Expository analysis

Sample 3:   Response to an article

Sample 4:   Personal narrative

Sample 5:   Analysis in a business letter

Science – Sample 1   Persuasive Response

Purpose

USING SCIENTIFIC INFORMATION TO PERSUADE
To persuade someone to improve his/her eating habits.

Assignment – This is a persuasive response from an anatomy and physiology class.

- The student supplies information about various problems/issues that affect the heart.
- The student chooses one issue and pretends an individual is in danger of this problem.
- The student persuades the reader to improve habit(s).

Step 1: Main Idea

Your current eating habits can lead to arteriosclerosis during which your artery walls will harden and thicken due to cholesterol and plaque.

Step 2: For Example

For example, you need to cut down on the French fries and the donuts. Fats and calcium can collect on the inner walls of your arteries. This makes it difficult for your blood to flow through your arteries.

Step 3: Why

The difficulty happens because the blood flow slows due to the blocked walls. This takes place with a build-up of fat and calcium over a long period of time. If some pieces of plaque break, you can have a stroke.

Step 4: Why of Why

Your diet is loaded with foods that contain high levels of saturated fats and trans fats. If the problem of arteriosclerosis exists and becomes severe, your heart might receive too little oxygen. You have told me that you have a mild form of diabetes; this makes you, especially, in danger.

Step 5: Why Important

Your eating habits are important because arteriosclerosis can result in your heart having to work too hard. The end consequence often is a heart attack that requires hospitalization.

Step 6: As a Result

As a result of changing your eating habits, you will be doing yourself a huge favor.

Science – Sample 1 (TEACHER'S NOTES)	Persuasive Response

Purpose

USING SCIENTIFIC INFORMATION TO PERSUADE
To persuade someone to improve his/her eating habits.

Assignment – This is a persuasive response from an anatomy and physiology class.

- The student interrelates scientific information with the point of view.
- The student provides a scientific explanation of "why."
- The student persuades through the "why" comments.

Step 1: Main Idea

The writer explains the relationship between the current behavior of his/her friend and the scientific reason for the issue being discussed.

Step 2: For Example

The example begins with an illustration that represents the eating practice of the friend. The writer, then, provides an example of how the friend's eating habits can lead to further problems.

Step 3: Why

The sentences in this section are short for greater impact. Each sentence contains a portion of scientific reasoning related to the issue. This approach is valuable with technical material; if the reader is placed on overload with too much information, the content is less effective.

Step 4: Why of Why

The first sentence becomes a secondary main idea statement with scientific information. Again, the writer wants to emphasize the reasoning "why" the restricted blood flow could become harmful.

Step 5: Why Important

This part represents the final "sell" of the idea. Without the previous information, these statements would not be powerful.

Step 6: As a Result

The final sentence is personal because the previous components of the response have been more scientific in nature. If the prior parts did not contain as much terminology, then this final sentence would need to be more technical.

Science – Sample 2   Expository Response

Purpose

THINKING ABOUT HOW SCIENCE AFFECTS US
To think about how people use science for change (both good and bad).

Assignment – This is an expository response based on the process of hormone injection in cattle.

- The student understands about farmers injecting hormones into cattle.
- The student describes how a group of people have reacted.
- The student discusses the behavior of the farmers and the protesters, but offers no opinion.

Step 1: Main Idea

A controversy exists as to whether it is safe to inject hormones into dairy cattle.

Step 2: For Example

For example, many farmers have decided that it is to their advantage to inject hormones into cattle in order to increase milk production. The FDA has stated that these hormone injections are safe for cattle and the consumer. However, there are several documented side effects on the cattle. These side effects range from cysts to leg injuries.

Step 3: Why

The farmers favor these injections because they increase milk production and profits. The protesters are against these injections because cattle receiving the injections wind up getting more diseases.

Step 4: Why of Why

The diseases cause farmers to give the cattle high levels of antibiotics that wind up in the cow's milk. The anti-injection group believes that people who drink lots of this genetically engineered milk will become resistant to antibiotics. Some of these people will become more susceptible to infection.

Step 5: Why Important

This controversy is important because the main government agency, the FDA, says the hormones are safe. On the other hand, certain scientists claim the hormone injections are dangerous.

Step 6: As a Result

As a result, further research needs to happen quickly so the consumer can be informed.

Science – Sample 2 (TEACHER'S NOTES)	Expository Response

Purpose

THINKING ABOUT HOW SCIENCE AFFECTS US
To think about how people use science for change (both good and bad).

Assignment – This is an expository response based on the process of hormone injection in cattle.

- The student explains the situation without taking stand.
- The student includes scientific terminology and information for support.
- The student discusses the impact of the science on one or more groups.

Step 1: Main Idea

The nature of the controversy is complex; therefore, the main idea needs to be simple and straightforward.

Step 2: For Example

The example component must clarify evidence for both sides. The sentences discuss one side and, then, the other. The sentence about the FDA establishes the credibility of one side of the controversy. By including the words "cysts" and "leg injuries" the other side gains credibility.

Step 3: Why

Again, the writer discusses one side and, then, the other in order to clarify the reasoning for both opponents. The words following each "because" present the prime reason why the injections are favored or opposed.

Step 4: Why of Why

There is no additional "why" necessary for those in favor; it is evident that their motive is profit. The further explanation of the position of those against the injection is valuable because the writer already has stated that the pro-injection side has the FDA's approval.

Step 5: Why Important

This section of the response reiterates the debate. The government indicates the injections are safe and some scientists do not.

Step 6: As a Result

This statement does not take a side. It presents a logical consequence, pointing out that the consumer is entitled to learn more.

Science – Sample 3	Response to Articles

Purpose

RELATING TEXT TO SELF THROUGH SCIENCE ARTICLES
To recognize the invention process and apply it to self.

Assignment – This is a response to articles completed in science class about invention.

- The student reads and discusses articles about four famous inventors.
- The student selects one or two adventures to discuss and relate to self.
- The student demonstrates an appreciation for scientific invention.

Step 1: Main Idea

Samuel Morse is one inventor who improved on ideas that already existed but were not originally well-developed.

Step 2: For Example

For example, Samuel Morse developed the "Morse Code" to improve the telegraph that already existed. He began thinking about this code after overhearing two scientists discussing problems with the telegraph on a voyage from England to the United States. The scientists discussed that the messages being sent over electrical wires were not clear.

Step 3: Why

Morse was interested, and he became curious about this problem; he started conducting experiments. Morse's curiosity led him to use a metal key that would touch a battery making a buzzer sound at the other end. However, the buzzer sounds created another problem.

Step 4: Why of Why

How would the person at the other end know what the message was saying? So, Morse created his code.

Step 5: Why Important

The experience of Morse is important to me because it reminds me of how I came up with my project for "The Invention Convention" when I was in the fifth grade. I heard a couple of kids in my class talking about the teacher being angry at their messy desks. I began thinking about their problem and came up with a desk organizer. The desk organizer could fit inside their desks; it was made of wood and had a place for pens, paper, books and other objects in the desk.

Step 6: As a Result

As a result of creating the desk organizer, I won a prize that I still have. One of the two students I heard talking used my invention for the rest of the school year.

Science – Sample 3 (TEACHER'S NOTES)	**Response to Articles**

Purpose

RELATING TEXT TO SELF THROUGH SCIENCE ARTICLES
To recognize the invention process and apply it to self.

Assignment – This is a response to articles completed in science class about invention.

- The student demonstrates both literal and inferential comprehension.
- The student explains why the science is/was so applicable.
- The student states a valid connection relating his/her experience to the science described as part of an article.

Step 1: Main Idea

This main idea shows an understanding of a theme embedded into the articles that were about inventors and scientists improving upon existing technology. The student selects one theme that he/she, also, can use to generate a valid connection later in the response.

Step 2: For Example

This example comes from one of the articles and illustrates the main idea. The student writes this part as a retelling of Morse's experience. The final sentence relates directly to the theme that prior knowledge existed.

Step 3: Why

This response is both literal and inferential. The idea of Morse's "curiosity" can be inferred from the text. The information about the metal key and wires is literally from the text.

Step 4: Why of Why

This "why of why" centers on the reason for Morse's curiosity. Why was he so interested in creating this code?

Step 5: Why Important

The student uses this section to develop his/her connection. "The experience of Morse is important to me because…." The connection must have a clear relationship to the rest of the response. The relationship here is established through the comments of the other students that led to the project. The student relates this step to self because the teacher required the connection. Otherwise, this step would center on the importance of Morse's invention.

Step 6: As a Result

The student briefly discusses the consequence of completing this project. The project won acclaim and was used practically.

Science – Sample 4   Personal Narrative

Purpose

DESCRIBING THINKING DURING AN EXPERIMENT
To discuss personal thought processes during an experiment.

Assignment – This is a personal narrative response based on experience related to the completion of a biology experiment.

- The student describes personal thoughts and feelings.
- The student uses appropriate terminology.
- The student demonstrates an understanding of the scientific process.

Step 1: Main Idea

I was both excited and relieved to find out that my hypothesis was correct. The hypothesis was as follows: If half of the pectinase and half of the cellulose are added, apple juice production will be more effective.

Step 2: For Example

For example, from the dependent variable, the amount of apple juice produced, I found that the maximum amount of juice can be made from the least amount of enzyme.

Step 3: Why

I figured that this would happen because the better the enzyme worked, the greater the quantity of juice.

Step 4: Why of Why

The enzyme acts as a stimulator that increases production, but I had to figure out the right amounts to add. At first, I was a little frustrated because I was worried that I would be adding enzymes forever without drawing any conclusions. However, after my second step, it became clear that the combination of half pectinase and half cellulose was going to be right.

Step 5: Why Important

Proving this hypothesis is important to a company because it will spend less money and produce more juice. If I were a chemist working at a juice company, I would save the company lots of money.

Step 6: As a Result

As a result of saving the company money, I might get a raise and be able to afford a sports car.

Thanks to Jake Greenwood, Ridgefield High School, Ridgefield CT for his assistance on this example.

Science – Sample 4 (TEACHER'S NOTES)	Personal Narrative

Purpose

DESCRIBING THINKING DURING AN EXPERIMENT
To discuss personal thought processes during an experiment.

Assignment – This is a personal narrative response based on experience related to the completion of a biology experiment.

- The student interplays his/her emotions with the scientific process.
- The student uses terminology as part of the narrative.
- The student discusses a valid application of the experience.

Step 1: Main Idea

The student relates his/her emotions to the hypothesis. This main idea could change but still be valid if the hypothesis were not supported; in this instance, the emotions would change. (I was disappointed to find out....)

Step 2: For Example

The example continues to use an aspect of the scientific process—the dependent variable. He/she describes information related to the dependent variable.

Step 3: Why

Ordinarily, the writer would never begin the statement with a pronoun. However, because this assignment is labeled as a narrative, the use of pronouns is accepted. The words "I figured" mean the same as a prediction.

Step 4: Why of Why

The student is answering the question: Why does a better-working enzyme result in a greater amount of juice? This is the direct "why of why" response—basing the thought questions on the specific words in the previous response.

Step 5: Why Important

This component is often the forgotten part of science experiments. Why is this information important to...? In this case: Why are the findings of this experiment important to a juice company?

Step 6: As a Result

This is a practical consequence that a young chemist might generate.

Science – Sample 5	Business Letter

Purpose

PRESENTING SCIENTIFIC INFORMATION FOR ACTION
To think about how pollution affects life in the water.

Assignment – This is a section from a business letter describing a community concern that relates to polluted and toxic waters.

- The letter is addressed to the governor of the state.
- The letter presents data and information derived from research and actual student testing conducted with water chemists.
- The letter needs to describe one scientific issue clearly. (A subsequent part of the response will present a viable solution.)

Step 1: Main Idea

The levels of dissolved oxygen in the bottom waters in the northeastern portion of the Sound are so low that life is endangered.

Step 2: For Example

For example, the oxygen level needs to be over 3 milligrams per liter for life to thrive in the bottom waters of the Sound. When tested last month the dissolved oxygen levels are below 3 milligrams per liter. In addition, the temperature of these bottom waters should be 12 degrees Centigrade for life to do well. The average temperature last month was 22.8 degrees Centigrade.

Step 3: Why

This data indicates that life in this area of the Sound is stressed because life depends upon an acceptable level of oxygen. The current low-level of oxygen indicates that this area has a condition called hypoxia.

Step 4: Why of Why

Hypoxia has a negative effect on the survival of existing life and reproduction. Hypoxia in this area reveals that the waters contain very high amounts of nitrogen. The high levels of nitrogen lead to the decay of algae; decaying algae is like a monster that sucks up huge amount of oxygen. Therefore, life, which is the food chain, has too little oxygen.

Step 5: Why Important

The current situation is important because the high levels of nitrogen are caused by the actions of people. Fertilizers and sewage running off into the waters create the problem.

Step 6: As a Result

As a result of this problem, aquatic life is destroyed and commercial industries are negatively affected.

Science – Sample 5 (TEACHER'S NOTES)	Business Letter

Purpose

PRESENTING SCIENTIFIC INFORMATION FOR ACTION
To think about how pollution affects life in the water.

Assignment – This is a section from a business letter describing the community concern that relates to polluted and toxic waters.

- The student presents scientific data.
- The student presents meaningful information so the audience understands essential concepts.
- The response employs relevant terminology.

Step 1: Main Idea

The writer presents one key term that piques the reader's interest. The location of the problem is specified and the consequence is given.

Step 2: For Example

The difficult terminology requires an in-depth explanation because the primary reader is not a scientist. This part of the response is designed to educate.

Step 3: Why

The reason discussed explains why the data in the previous part is necessary to consider. The writer includes the new term "hypoxia" in order to further the reader's understanding.

Step 4: Why of Why

The term "hypoxia" becomes the anchor for further explanation of scientific information that explains why this is a problem. The writer uses the comparative of decaying algae to a monster in order to get the point across. This type of comparative would not be effective if it were presented earlier in the text.

Step 5: Why Important

This part of the response connects the science to the reality that people are responsible. The connection allows the reader to grasp the idea that the problem can be solved because it is people who created the issue.

Step 6: As a Result

The consequences are negative; this statement would not be effective if the previous data and scientific information were not presented.

Part 3

Structuring a Response to a Social Studies Text, Article, Video or Research Question

Situation 1: Comparing Perspectives

The students have been studying events leading up to the Civil War. The students are going to spend most of the next week reading, viewing biographies, and discussing Abraham Lincoln. As an introduction, the students have just read an article about the *Lincoln Douglas Debates*. In addition, the students have read Lincoln's famous *house divided speech*.

The teacher has spent class time reading and discussing both sources. After the discussion, the teacher asks the students to apply the six-step Structured Writing process to a specific focus.

Focus: The key difference between Lincoln and Douglas on slavery

The students already understand the process. The students are allowed to use the article when recording their responses to the steps in the structure. However, except for quotations, the students are not allowed to copy information from either source.

☞   **Keep this in mind**:   Social studies is the perfect content to incorporate
                                          information from multiple sources into analytical
                                          paragraphs.

Here's one example of using the six steps of Structured Writing.

Step 1:

In the "main idea," the student describes the major difference presented in the content. With this "main idea," the student is citing the central issue being described in the sources. The student could write about this issue in one sentence; however, the student realizes that it is clearer to state the issue in two sentences. Therefore, the main idea in this instance is actually two sentences.

Main Idea   Stephen Douglas, the existing U.S. Senator from Illinois, believed that
                            the government in Washington should try to broker a peaceful solution
                            to the issue of slavery. Lincoln wanted the voters of Illinois to
                            understand the dangers of any compromise.

Step 2:

In the "for example," the student presents the fact that Douglas sponsored the Kansas-Nebraska Act. To show Lincoln's position, the student uses a quotation from the "house divided" speech to elaborate on the main idea. When placing the six responses into a paragraph, the student might cross out the words "for example" in order to improve word flow. However, it is better to lead with this phrase during the process of writing the rough draft because the student stays more focused.

For Example	For example, in 1854 Douglas sponsored the Kansas-Nebraska Act. This act did not prevent the spread of slavery to new territories. During his "house divided" speech, Lincoln commented on the failure of this act. "Under the operation of that policy, that agitation has only not ceased, but has constantly augmented."

Step 3:

The student explains "why" Lincoln stated these words. In addition, the student states "why" Douglas was in favor of the Kansas-Nebraska Act. The explanation needs to have some level of depth which shows the student understands the central concepts of the readings. The student poses a simple "why" question to aid in completing this part of the writing and thinking process. The same premise holds for the "why of why" component.

"Why" Question	Why did Lincoln comment on the failure of the act?
Why	Lincoln commented on the failure of the act because he believed that a nation split on an emotional issue, like slavery, could not survive. Douglas, on the other hand, believed that he could help to broker a compromise on the issue.

Step 4:

The student poses another "why" question to aid in completing this part of the writing and thinking process. The student picks a phrase from the third step to use as an anchor in the question for this part of the process. The student chooses the phrase "broker a compromise" to be incorporated in the question.

Why of Why Question	Why did Lincoln not see a possible brokered compromise?
Why of Why	Lincoln believed that a brokered compromise was impossible because of the Dred Scott case. In this case the Supreme Court ruled that Congress could not stop slavery from spreading into territories. Lincoln believed that these territories would get more and more violent.

Step 5:

The "why important" requires the student to tell the significance of the problem. In this case, the student centers on the significance of why this speech was so important to Lincoln.

Why Important   The "house divided" speech was important because it made Lincoln's beliefs about slavery clear. Lincoln makes it clear that the United States must stop being divided on this emotional issue.

Step 6:

In the "as a result," the student states the consequence or consequences. The student relates the response to this step to the previous sentences.

As a Result   As a result, Lincoln kept this position when he was elected President two years later.

By writing these six parts continuously, the student has created an in-depth response that meets these criteria.

- The responses analytical.
- The response focuses on opposing points of view.
- The response explains the relation of the quotation and information to the points of view.
- The response is organized.
- The response makes a valid connection.

The six responses of the Structured Writing process become one or two rough draft paragraphs. Here are the six responses by the student who learned about the *Lincoln and Douglas debates*.

Step 1   Stephen Douglas, the existing U.S. Senator from Illinois, believed that the government in Washington should try to broker a peaceful solution to the issue of slavery. Lincoln wanted the voters of Illinois to understand the dangers of any compromise.

Step 2   For example, in 1854 Douglas sponsored the Kansas-Nebraska Act. This act did not prevent the spread of slavery to new territories. During his "house divided" speech, Lincoln commented on the failure of this act. "Under the operation of that policy, that agitation has only not ceased, but has constantly augmented."

Step 3   Lincoln commented on the failure of the act because he believed that a nation split on an emotional issue, like slavery, could not survive. Douglas, on the other hand, believed that he could help to broker a compromise on the issue.

Step 4   Lincoln believed that a brokered compromise was impossible because of the Dred Scott case. In this case the Supreme Court ruled that Congress could not stop slavery from spreading into territories. Lincoln believed that these territories would get more and more violent.

Step 5   The "house divided" speech was important because it made Lincoln's beliefs about slavery clear. Lincoln makes it clear that the United States must stop being divided on this emotional issue.

Step 6   As a result, Lincoln kept this position when he was elected President two years later.

Because of the length, the student can break the six responses into two rough draft paragraphs. Steps one, two and three become one paragraph; the remaining three steps form a second paragraph of the response. The paragraphs should reveal that the student possesses an understanding of the article at these comprehension levels: literal, synthesis, and inferential.

Paragraph 1 (steps 1, 2, and 3)

Stephen Douglas, the existing U.S. Senator from Illinois, believed that the government in Washington should try to broker a peaceful solution to the issue of slavery. Lincoln wanted the voters of Illinois to understand the dangers of any compromise. For example, in 1854 Douglas sponsored the Kansas-Nebraska Act. This act did not prevent the spread of slavery to new territories. During his "house divided" speech, Lincoln commented on the failure of this act. "Under the operation of that policy, that agitation has only not ceased, but has constantly augmented." Lincoln commented on the failure of the act because he believed that a nation split on an emotional issue, like slavery, could not survive. Douglas, on the other hand, believed that he could help to broker a compromise on the issue.

Paragraph 2 (steps 2, 3, and 4)

Lincoln believed that a brokered compromise was impossible because of the Dred Scott case. In this case the Supreme Court ruled that Congress could not stop slavery from spreading into territories. Lincoln believed that these territories would get more and more violent. The "house divided" speech was important because it made Lincoln's beliefs about slavery clear. Lincoln makes it clear that the United States must stop being divided on this emotional issue. As a result, Lincoln kept this position when he was elected President two years later.

Situation 2: Exploring Cause and Consequence

The students have read two articles discussing the historical conflict between India and Pakistan. These articles are part of a unit centering on "Conflicts Around The World."

The teacher has spent class time reading and discussing the articles. After the discussion, the teacher asked the students to apply the six-step Structured Writing process to a specific focus.

Focus: **the historical reason for the conflict**

The students already understand the step-by-step writing process. The students are allowed to use the articles when recording their responses to the steps in the structure. However, except for quotations, the students are not allowed to copy information from either source; in this assignment the inclusion of a quotation is not required.

☞   **Keep this in mind:** Causes and consequences interact constantly.

Here's one example of a student's set of responses.

Step 1:

In the "main idea," the student describes the major reason presented in the content. With this "main idea," the student is citing a central issue being described in the sources. The student can write about this issue in one sentence.

Main Idea   The conflict between India and Pakistan started when the Indian government became outraged that the Pakistani government interfered with the independence of Kashmir.

Step 2:

In the "for example," the student presents the fact that Kashmir was given the option of remaining independent. To clarify the situation, the student briefly discusses the separation of territories after the British gave up rule. When placing the six responses into a paragraph, the student might cross out the words "for example" in order to improve word flow. However, it is better to lead with this phrase during the process of because the student stays more focused.

For Example   For example, the British had ruled the territory that is now India and Pakistan. When the British gave up control of the territories in 1947, most of the territory became an independent India. Land that was occupied by a majority of Muslims became Pakistan. The area called Kashmir had the option of remaining independent. When the leaders of the new Pakistan interfered with the Maharaja of Kashmir's decision to remain independent, India responded.

Step 3:

The student explains "why" India became outraged. In addition, the student thinks about "why" Pakistan wanted Kashmir. The explanation needs have some level of depth which shows the student understands the central concepts of the readings. The student poses a simple "why" question to aid in completing this part of the writing and thinking process. The same premise holds for the "why of why" component.

"Why" Question	Why did Pakistan want Kashmir to join it?
Why	Pakistan wanted to convince Kashmir to join it because most people in Kashmir were Muslim, even though its leaders were Sikh. The Indian government was willing to go along with the original idea to let Kashmir decide for itself. However, the Indian government thought of Pakistan's interference as illegal.

Step 4:

The student poses another "why" question to aid in completing this part of the writing and thinking process. The student picks a phrase from the third step to use as an anchor in the question for this part of the process. The student chooses the phrase "interference as illegal" to be incorporated in the question.

Why of Why	Why did the Indians look at this interference as illegal?
Why of Why	The Indian government looked at the action by Pakistan as illegal. The original treaty set up when the British gave up power called for the territory of Kashmir to decide on its own if it was going to join one of the two countries or remain independent. Before Pakistan's interference, the Maharaja, Kashmir had decided to be independent. Now the Maharaja chose to join India for protection from Pakistan.

Step 5:

The "why important" requires the student to tell the significance of the problem. In this case, the student centers on the significance of why this conflict is important.

Why Important	This conflict is important because the newly formed Indian government declared war on Pakistan to drive Pakistani forces from Kashmir. This conflict that began decades ago is still continuing. The conflict is even more serious because both India and Pakistan have nuclear arms.

Step 6:

In the "as a result," the student states the consequence or consequences. The student relates the response to this step to the previous sentences.

As a Result   As a result, neither side has been willing to take the first step in settling this dispute even though there are major possible consequences.

The student has created an in-depth response that meets these criteria.

- The responses analytical.
- The response supports the main idea.
- The response explains the issue.
- The response is organized.
- The response makes a valid consequence.

The six responses of the Structured Writing process become one or two rough draft paragraphs. Here are the six responses by the student who learned about the *India and Pakistan conflict.*

Step 1   The conflict between India and Pakistan started when the Indian government became outraged that the Pakistani government interfered with the independence of Kashmir.

Step 2   For example, the British had ruled the territory that is now India and Pakistan. When the British gave up control of the territories in 1947, most of the territory became an independent India. Land that was occupied by a majority of Muslims became Pakistan. The area called Kashmir had the option of remaining independent. When the leaders of the new Pakistan interfered with the Maharaja of Kashmir's decision to remain independent, India responded.

Step 3   Pakistan wanted to convince Kashmir to join it because most people in Kashmir were Muslim, even though its leaders were Sikh. The Indian government was willing to go along with the original idea to let Kashmir decide for itself. However, the Indian government thought of Pakistan's interference as illegal.

Step 4   The Indian government looked at the action by Pakistan as illegal. The original treaty set up when the British gave up power called for the territory of Kashmir to decide on its own if it was going to join one of the two countries or remain independent. Before Pakistan's interference, the Maharaja, Kashmir had decided to be independent. Now the Maharaja chose to join India for protection from Pakistan.

Step 5 This conflict is important because the newly formed Indian government declared war on Pakistan to drive Pakistani forces from Kashmir. This conflict that began decades ago is still continuing. The conflict is even more serious because both India and Pakistan have nuclear arms.

Step 6 As a result, neither side has been willing to take the first step in settling this dispute even though there are major possible consequences.

Because of the length, the student can break the six responses into three rough draft paragraphs. Steps one and two become one paragraph because the response in the second step is very lengthy; steps three and four form a second paragraph of the response; steps five and six provide a final, short paragraph.

Paragraph 1 (steps 1 and 2)

The conflict between India and Pakistan started when the Indian government became outraged that the Pakistani government interfered with the independence of Kashmir. For example, the British had ruled the territory that is now India and Pakistan. When the British gave up control of the territories in 1947, most of the territory became an independent India. Land that was occupied by a majority of Muslims became Pakistan. The area called Kashmir had the option of remaining independent. When the leaders of the new Pakistan interfered with the Maharaja of Kashmir's decision to remain independent, India responded.

Paragraph 2 (steps 3 and 4)

Pakistan wanted to convince Kashmir to join it because most people in Kashmir were Muslim, even though its leaders were Sikh. The Indian government was willing to go along with the original idea to let Kashmir decide for itself. However, the Indian government thought of Pakistan's interference as illegal. The Indian government looked at the action by Pakistan as illegal. The original treaty set up when the British gave up power called for the territory of Kashmir to decide on its own if it was going to join one of the two countries or remain independent. Before Pakistan's interference, the Maharaja, Kashmir had decided to be independent. Now the Maharaja chose to join India for protection from Pakistan.

Paragraph 3 (steps 5 and 6)

This conflict is important because the newly formed Indian government declared war on Pakistan to drive Pakistani forces from Kashmir. This conflict that began decades ago is still continuing. The conflict is even more serious because both India and Pakistan have nuclear arms. As a result, neither side has been willing to take the first step in settling this dispute even though there are major possible consequences.

Teachers can evaluate the six steps of the rough draft according to the rubric on the following page.

Structured Writing Rubric – Social Studies

Student			Teacher		Comment
Yes	No	The main idea is clear.	Yes	No	_____
Yes	No	The "for example" is complete, explaining one event or situation.	Yes	No	_____
Yes	No	The "why" explains the cause of the action discussed in the example.	Yes	No	_____
Yes	No	The first three parts of the paragraph are logical.	Yes	No	_____
Yes	No	The "why of why" provides additional insight.	Yes	No	_____
Yes	No	The "why important" clearly states the significance.	Yes	No	_____
Yes	No	The action of the event is broken down.	Yes	No	_____
Yes	No	The "as a result" is a logical consequence that relates to the importance.	Yes	No	_____
Yes	No	The entire first draft paragraph is coherent.	Yes	No	_____
Yes	No	The student applies editing and revising skills.	Yes	No	_____

Student Comment: _____

_____

Teacher Comment: _____

_____

Applying the Structured Writing Process

SOCIAL STUDIES

On the pages that follow are several different applications of the Structured Writing process tailored for social studies classes. Each sample contains the objective or purpose and a description of the assignment in addition to each of the six steps.

There are two listings for each sample, one contains the student responses for each of the six steps and the second contains the teacher notes for each step. Samples with teacher notes have the words "teacher notes" at the top of the page.

The following are samples for Social Studies classes.

Sample 1:   Persuasive response

Sample 2:   Expository analysis

Sample 3:   Analysis of a chapter or section of a book

Sample 4:   Personal narrative

Sample 5:   Historical response in a letter

Social Studies – Sample 1	**Persuasive Response**

Purpose

TAKING A POSITION ON A CURRENT ISSUE
To specify reasons for or against a particular issue.

Assignment – This is a persuasive response from a social studies class.

- The student presents a position and one reason why other should agree.
- The student discusses facts to persuade the reader and embed facts into the text.
- The student states arguments logically.

Step 1: Main Idea

The death penalty needs to be ended because the legal system sometimes is corrupt as it was in the case of Anthony Graves.

Step 2: For Example

For example, the case of Anthony Graves reveals that prosecuting attorneys withheld key information at Graves' original trial in 1994 for multiple murders in Texas. In addition, the prosecutors convinced witnesses to present uncertain testimony as the truth. Finally, there was no physical evidence presented at the trial linking Graves to the murders.

Step 3: Why

This situation happened because prosecutors believed the real killer who told them that Graves was an accomplice. Six years later, this individual informed prosecutors that he lied about Graves who had nothing to do with the murders. Prosecutors refused to believe him.

Step 4: Why of Why

Prosecutors refused to believe the real murderer's changed story because they did not want to be embarrassed. It took another six years for pro bono lawyers to get the Court Of Appeals to grant another trial for Graves.

Step 5: Why Important

The case of Anthony Graves is important because it shows that, at times, prosecutors want to convict someone and, themselves, break the law. If Graves had been executed, there would not have been an appeal. When people reflect on their position related to the death penalty, it is crucial for them to think of this man's fate.

Step 6: As a Result

As a result of appeal, Graves was freed on October 27, 2010. This was sixteen years after he was falsely convicted. In the last thirty years, over one hundred people on death row have been found innocent and released from jail.

Social Studies – Sample 1 (TEACHER'S NOTES)   Persuasive Response

Purpose

TAKING A POSITION ON A CURRENT ISSUE
To specify reasons for or against a particular issue.

Assignment – This is a persuasive response from a social studies class.

- The student needs to show literal and inferential understanding of the topic.
- The student needs to embed information into his/her point of view.
- The student needs to explain the reason(s) for his/her position.

Step 1: Main Idea

The main idea is based on one theme presented in the articles read. The writer has chosen to focus on one case rather than a few cases that deal with corruption.

Step 2: For Example

This information supports the idea of corruption presented in the main idea. Each of the three details builds the writer's case. If the writer had chosen the opposite point of view, a totally different set of supporting information would be included.

Step 3: Why

The writer includes "why" the prosecution was able to make its case and "why" the prosecution's behavior is corrupt.

Step 4: Why of Why

Because this is a persuasive piece, the writer can present evaluative comments. "...they did not want to be embarrassed...." is evaluative. The second sentence is information to validate the evaluative comment.

Step 5: Why Important

In this type of persuasive piece, the "why important" component is the clincher—the part of the response that gains audience acceptance of the writer's point of view. The statement that begins: "If Graves had been executed...." is the bottom line of the writer's perspective.

Step 6: As a Result

The statement of consequence offers the result of Graves not being executed. The writer adds a powerful follow-up statement about the time Graves had to serve in prison and that Graves is not the only one exposed to this fate.

Social Studies – Sample 2   Expository Analysis

Purpose

PRESENTING HISTORICAL INFORMATION
To develop a basic analysis that one event, belief or action.

Assignment – This is an expository analysis after discussing an event.

- The student has read the text and watched a short streaming video.
- The student focuses on one main idea related the material.
- The student includes relevant facts and analyzes these facts.

Step 1: Main Idea

During the American Revolution, members of the Continental Congress created a weak national government through the Articles of Confederation. This document caused debate.

Step 2: For Example

For example, the Articles of Confederation in 1777 prohibited the national government from having an army and levying taxes. In addition, there was no President or judicial branch. Even with a weak set of articles, there were still debates, such as who would control western lands; this debate actually resulted in the federal government controlling these lands.

Step 3: Why

The debates occurred because some leaders feared that a strong central government could lead to another monarchy. Others feared that if the states had too much power, a state could decide to eliminate certain rights that were supposed to be part of the new country.

Step 4: Why of Why

This fear caused a lot of concern for those who wanted a strong national government and those who wanted a weak one. The American Revolution was going on and people could not stop worrying about another tyrant, like King George. Some people were concerned that if the colonists won the war, certain states with more resources and more people might decide to form their own country.

Step 5: Why Important

The Articles of Confederation were important because the document set down ideas about which all thirteen colonies agreed until 1789.

Step 6: As a Result

As a result, the United States was ready for a more in-depth Constitution in 1789.

| Social Studies – Sample 2 (TEACHER'S NOTES) | Expository Analysis |

Purpose

PRESENTING HISTORICAL INFORMATION
To develop a basic analysis that one event, belief or action.

Assignment – This is an expository analysis after discussing an event.

- The student demonstrates literal and synthesis comprehension.
- The student explains the issue without showing bias.
- The student shows an understanding of the historical times.

Step 1: Main Idea

This main idea statement is not an opinion because the Articles really were weak. The main idea only can represent an opinion in a persuasive piece.

Step 2: For Example

This segment presents a sequence of facts that support the idea of the weak central government. The writer, also, includes the idea that certain proposals caused controversy.

Step 3: Why

This "why" component is the cornerstone of understanding the information. The reasons for these selected debates hits at the heart of the conflicting beliefs.

Step 4: Why of Why

Why did the fear on both sides matter? The information in this part of the response presents the analysis necessary to demonstrate an understanding of the historical times. Without this section, the response is incomplete.

Step 5: Why Important

Even though ideas for the Articles were debated, the significance of the document is stated clearly. Because steps 3 and 4 are so complete, this segment does not need as much depth.

Step 6: As a Result

The statement in the "as a result" shows a heightened connection between the Articles and the Constitution.

Social Studies – Sample 3	**Response to a Chapter in a Book**

Purpose

RELATING TEXT AND OUTSIDE READING
To combine information and discuss the viewpoint of the outside reading.

Assignment – This is a response to a chapter in a book about "Shay's Rebellion."[*]

- The student reads the text and, then, a related reading on the topic.
- The student discusses the viewpoint of the author.
- The student includes relevant facts from text and the outside reading.

Step 1: Main Idea

Steven Gillon believes that Shay's Rebellion had a major influence on the support of American leaders for the Constitution.

Step 2: For Example

For example, even those who were not the strongest supporters of revolution were upset by the rebellion of the farmers. The author discusses how those who supported rebellion against the British were worried that the protests of the farmers would cause "mob" rule.

Step 3: Why

These leaders were worried about mob rule because the new government could only work if authority were respected. Gillon writes the following: "They believed the central question facing the young republic was how to balance the demands of democracy with the need to preserve social order." (page 37)

Step 4: Why of Why

The leaders believed this because the United States was very fragile and one major insurrection could tear the country apart. The Articles of Confederation did not create the power for the national government to order troops to resist.

Step 5: Why Important

Shay's Rebellion was important to the supporters of the Constitution because they could make the case that a weak central government could lead to lots of these rebellions. In the future, the rebellions might not be led by farmers, but by any group that was unhappy.

Step 6: As a Result

As a result of this concern, the supporters of a strong Constitution were able to make a case for Congress being able to create an army and levy taxes to pay for it.

[*]10 Days That Unexpectedly Changed America, Steven Gillon, New York: Three Rivers Press, 2006.

Social Studies – Sample 3 (TEACHER'S NOTES)	Response to a Chapter in a Book

Purpose

RELATING TEXT AND OUTSIDE READING
To combine information and discuss the viewpoint of the outside reading.

Assignment – This is a response to a chapter in a book about "Shay's Rebellion."[*]

- The student comprehends the author's viewpoint.
- The student incorporates this viewpoint clearly.
- The student organizes information in a logical manner.

Step 1: Main Idea

The main idea reflects the author's theme and the relationship of that theme to historical events.

Step 2: For Example

The writer has a lot of information from which to choose. He/she selects the concern about "mob rule" because this was on the minds of Americans from different political perspectives; it was a unifying concern.

Step 3: Why

The writer uses the quote to clarify the author's reason why this concern was so great. There were other quotes to select, but this one hits on the idea of balancing democracy and social order.

Step 4: Why of Why

This component is inferential; the writer has drawn an appropriate conclusion from the text. The second sentence supports the inference and is factual in nature.

Step 5: Why Important

The first part of this segment represents the thinking of the author and the main idea. The second part of the response is another inference from the writer who extends the author's thinking one step farther.

Step 6: As a Result

This statement is the conclusion of the author; the writer has synthesized a sequence of statements by the author.

[*]10 Days That Unexpectedly Changed America, Steven Gillon, New York: Three Rivers Press, 2006.

Social Studies – Sample 4   Personal Narrative

Purpose

DEMONSTRATING EMPATHY AND APPRECIATION
To take on the role of a historical figure.

Assignment – This is a personal narrative paragraph based on the behavior of a historical figure.

The student pretends to be Teddy Roosevelt in 1917.

- The student describes personal thoughts and feelings.
- The student shows an appreciation for events and behaviors.
- The student attempts to show the cause(s) for behavior(s).

Step 1: Main Idea

My love for nature leads me to support the idea of conservation of our land and our resources for the benefit of current and future generations.

Step 2: For Example

For example, I have set aside 150 million acres of land as a forest preserve. I have begun projects to construct dams across the west, such as in Arizona. I supported the Newsland Acts (1902) that helped to protect our waters. I helped to create the Grand Canyon National Monument which later became Grand Canyon National Park.

Step 3: Why

I have set aside the forestlands because much of our national forests have been destroyed. In fact, three-quarters of our forests have disappeared during the past century. I have undertaken irrigation projects because too much of our waterways are becoming controlled by private parties. I have supported the Grand Canyon National Monument in order to prevent private concerns from building a railroad around the rim of the Canyon.

Step 4: Why of Why

I have done these actions because "our duty to the whole, including the unborn generations, bids us restrain an unprincipled present-day minority from wasting the heritage of these unborn generations." (1916)

Step 5: Why Important

This heritage is important because failure to conserve our natural resources would deprive our grandchildren from experiencing America's beauty.

Step 6: As a Result

As a result of conservation, future generations will be able to enjoy places like Crater National Park in Oregon.

Social Studies – Sample 4 (TEACHER'S NOTES)	**Personal Narrative**

Purpose

DEMONSTRATING EMPATHY AND APPRECIATION
To take on the role of a historical figure.

Assignment – This is a personal narrative paragraph based on the behavior of a historical figure.

The student pretends to be Teddy Roosevelt in 1917.

- The student demonstrates an understanding of relevant events.
- The student presents supporting information about the main idea only.
- The student assumes the character of the figure.

Step 1: Main Idea

This main idea is simply stated but represents a major goal of the Roosevelt administration

Step 2: For Example

The details in this section are taken from Roosevelt's life. The writer has the license to choose policy from different years. Each part of the example does support the main idea. The information is taken from different sources.

Step 3: Why

There is a one-to-one correspondence between each part of the example and each reason why. The first sentence in this section relates to the first sentence in the "example" section. The specific nature of the responses show the writer understands relevant information.

Step 4: Why of Why

The writer selects this quote to bring some of Roosevelt's language into the response. The quote is from 1916, but the writer has literary license. The key phrase in the quote is "wasting the heritage."

Step 5: Why Important

This segment of the response is straightforward. The impact idea here is embedded in the phrase "failure to conserve."

Step 6: As a Result

The concluding sentence brings in an actual location to refocus the reading on the notion that Roosevelt's vision of conservation is comprised of real places that future generations will be able to visit.

Social Studies – Sample 5	Response in a Letter

Purpose

DETERMINING WHY A HISTORICAL FIGURE BEHAVES IN A PARTICULAR WAY
To evaluate the behavior and actions of important historical figures.

Assignment – This is a response in a letter describing advice that one historical figure might give another.

Letter from John Winthrop, leader of the Massachusetts Bay Colony, to Roger Williams, minister and dissident who fled to found Rhode Island.

- The letter demonstrates an understanding of events.
- The student takes a point of view that is logical to events and actions.
- The student shows and understanding of circumstances that caused events.

Step 1: Main Idea

I appreciate your point of view about the separation of church and state, but I cannot support this belief.

Step 2: For Example

For example, our laws in the Massachusetts Bay Colony are based largely on religious practices. Our colony was founded on the premise that these religiously based laws guide people in their daily lives.

Step 3: Why

This guidance exists because the people of the colony need a common bond to help them survive the difficulties of life in Massachusetts. People need a set of moral ideas that encourage them to act as a community.

Step 4: Why of Why

People must act as a community because they need to depend upon each other.

Step 5: Why Important

Preventing a separation of church and state is important because differing views will destroy unity. The secular laws will provide a different message from the religious laws.

Step 6: As a Result

As a result of these differences, dissention will occur and people will start to form cliques that will destroy the unity.

Social Studies – Sample 5 (TEACHER'S NOTES)	Response in a Letter

Purpose

DETERMINING WHY A HISTORICAL FIGURE BEHAVES IN A PARTICULAR WAY
To evaluate the behavior and actions of important historical figures.

Assignment – This is a response in a letter describing advice that one historical figure might give another.

Letter from John Winthrop, leader of the Massachusetts Bay Colony, to Roger Williams, minister and dissident who fled to found Rhode Island.

- The student shows the relationship between actions and events.
- The student represents the point of view of the figure.
- The student embeds historical information so that cause and effect are clear.

Step 1: Main Idea

The main idea centers on an admiration that Winthrop had for Williams but a perspective on what was necessary for the Colony to survive.

Step 2: For Example

The example is designed to remind Williams of the purpose/goal of the Colony and to hint that his points of view do not meet that goal.

Step 3: Why

The "why" centers on the logic that Winthrop believed to be true. A community can only survive if there is unity in purpose and thought. Williams' beliefs undermined this unity. The writer makes this point clearly.

Step 4: Why of Why

This segment is the real bottom line; Winthrop hopes that Williams will "see the light."

Step 5: Why Important

Winthrop worried that the secular laws would bring disharmony and corruption. Williams believed this separation would bring a greater understanding. The writer uses this statement to appeal one final time. The word "important" becomes an opportunity for the reader to rethink his position.

Step 6: As a Result

The consequence is the conclusion that Winthrop wants to bring home.

Part 4

Structuring a Response to a Mathematical Skill or Process

Why write paragraphs during math instruction?

Communication is the name of the game. The success of our students depends upon their ability to provide in-depth analysis for every content area. Often communication in mathematics is limited to a sequence of numbers and symbols that represent problem solution. However, if students cannot present logical explanations of required mathematical processing, they will be unable to apply learned skills to a variety of realistic situations.

Writing paragraphs about mathematics allows students to develop more logical and in-depth mathematical thinking. As students write, they increase their understanding of processes and the reasons why they apply certain skills. Written paragraphs teach students to justify their reasoning and to reflect on the importance of certain steps required to solve problems. Utilizing the six steps of the Structured Writing process provide students with the opportunity to reflect about the concept and mathematic principle being explored. In addition, students become comfortable applying mathematical terminology to their explanations; this results in heightened comprehension.

By increasing proficiency in communicating mathematical processing with peers, students are clarifying their own thinking about how to solve a particular problem. Students learn to explain their problem-solving approaches through their paragraphs; their peers, then, can evaluate the validity and logic of the responses. As students record each part of the paragraph, they personally evaluate their own knowledge of the topic and assess if their explanation communicates the proper message.

Students need to write well-designed mathematical paragraphs to enhance their own understanding of concepts through reflection. In addition, students need to construct paragraphs in order to share their critical thinking with others. The quality of these explanations is essential if mathematics is to be utilized and appreciated by the student as he or she matures. Formal assessments include math prompts because experts agree that this ability to communicate coherently is a required skill for the twenty-first century and beyond.

> **On a personal note...**
> In the 1980s, I wrote a series entitled Math And Writing which was published by Educators Publishing Service.

Situation 1: Using Math to Make Personal Decisions

The students have been learning about keeping a monthly budget and making personal economic decisions. The teacher has created a hypothetical scenario in which a wage earner has to decide which of two jobs will allow him to save enough money for a down payment on a home. The teacher presents the following situation.

A twenty-six year old, named Mary, has recently completed a graduate program in Engineering. She has to decide which of two job offers to accept. She likes both companies equally; either company will offer her good opportunity for advancement and interesting projects. Mary's determining factor will be based on which company's salary over five years will allow her to save more money for a down payment on a house. Both companies have offered her a contract that guaranteed employment for five years.

The Jones Engineering Company has offered Mary a starting salary of $72,000 per year. In addition, she would receive a bonus of $2,500 if she went to work there. The Personnel Director at Jones promised her that she would be guaranteed a 5% salary increase each year. At Jones, she would have to pay $150 per month toward her health insurance premium.

The Smithson Engineering Company has offered Mary a starting salary of $65,000 per year. With Smithson, she would receive a signing bonus of $5,000 if she went to work there. This Personnel Director promised her that she would receive a yearly salary increase of 6% per year for the first five years. In addition, Mary is guaranteed another bonus of $5,000 after her fourth year of work. She does not have to pay for health insurance.

Mary has determined that it would cost her $70,000 per year to live and pay Federal, state, and local taxes. She plans to save any earnings over $70,000 to put toward a down payment on a house in five years.

The teacher has spent class time discussing this type of math application. After the discussion, the teacher asks the students to apply the six-step Structured Writing process to a specific focus.

Focus: the company for whom Mary should work

The students already understand the required mathematical process. The students are allowed to use their notes when determining their responses to each of the steps in the writing structure.

Each student is expected to create a chart showing the amount saved per year at each engineering company.

Jones Engineering Company

	Earnings/Bonus	Expenses	Insurance	Saved
Bonus	$ 2,500			$ 2,500
Year 1	$72,000	$70,000	($1,800)	$ 200
Year 2	$75,600	$70,000	($1,800)	$ 3,800
Year 3	$79,380	$70,000	($1,800)	$ 7,580
Year 4	$83,349	$70,000	($1,800)	$11,549
Year 5	$87,526	$70,000	($1,800)	$15,716
Total				$41,345

Smithson Engineering Company

	Earnings/Bonus	Expenses	Insurance	Saved
Bonus	$ 5,000			$ 5,000
Year 1	$65,000	$70,000	0	($ 5,000)
Year 2	$68,900	$70,000	0	($ 1,100)
Year 3	$73,034	$70,000	0	$ 3,034
Year 4	$77,416	$70,000	0	$ 7,416
Bonus	$ 5,000			$ 5,000
Year 5	$82,061	$70,000	0	$12,061
Total				$26,411

Here is one example of the student's response using the six steps.

Step 1:

In the "main idea," the student describes the major difference presented in the content. With this "main idea," the student is citing the central issue being described in the sources. The student can write about this issue in one sentence.

Main Idea   Mary will be able to save $15,000 more by accepting the position at Jones Engineering.

Step 2:

In the "for example," the student discusses the math that shows Mary being able to save money during her first year of employment at one company but not at the other company.

| For Example | At Jones, her yearly salary begins above the $70,000 that she needs to pay for yearly expenses, even with the insurance payment subtracted from her income. At Smithson, Mary will lose $5,000 her first year. She will have to use her bonus to make up the difference. In fact, Mary will lose money in her second year at Smithson, also. |

Step 3:

The student explains "why" she will be able to save money at one company versus the other.

| "Why" Question | Why will she save money at one company and not at the other? |

| Why | Mary will be able to save money immediately at Jones Engineering because her first year salary is more than $1,800 above the money she needs to pay her bills. At Smithson, her initial salary is $5,000 below the money required to pay her bills. Thus, she will have to use her bonus to break even. The higher percentage of increase at Smithson is not enough to make up the difference. |

Step 4:

The student poses another "why" question to aid in completing this part of the writing and thinking process. The student picks a phrase from the third step to use as an anchor in the question for this part of the process. The student chooses the phrase "percentage of increase" to be incorporated in the question.

| Why of Why | Why doesn't the higher percentage of increase help to catch up the Smithson salary? |

| Why of Why | The Smithson salary is to too far below the Jones starting salary for the extra one percent of increase to make much of a difference. The two salaries after five years are closer than expected because of the second bonus of $5,000 from Smithson. |

Step 5:

The "why important" requires the student to tell the significance of the problem. In this case, the student centers on the significance of why it is important for Mary to do the math before accepting one of the positions.

| Why Important | Calculating the math is important to Mary because she might easily be fooled by the higher bonuses at Smithson. Therefore, she might think |

she will save more at Smithson, even if she realized the first year salary loss of $5,000.

Step 6:

In the "as a result," the student states the consequence or consequences. The student relates the response to this step to the previous sentences.

As a Result   As a result, of completing the math charts, Mary can easily recognize that she can start saving money for her house in the first year if she accepts the position at Jones Engineering.

By writing these six parts continuously, the student has created an in-depth response that meets these criteria.

- The response is analytical.
- The response presents supporting data.
- The response explains the reason for the choice.
- The response is organized.
- The response connects to a valid life experience.

The six responses of the Structured Writing process become one or two paragraphs.

Step 1   Mary will be able to save $15,000 more by accepting the position at Jones Engineering.

Step 2   At Jones, her yearly salary begins above the $70,000 that she needs to pay for yearly expenses, even with the insurance payment subtracted from her income. At Smithson, Mary will lose $5,000 her first year. She will have to use her bonus to make up the difference. In fact, Mary will lose money in her second year at Smithson, also.

Step 3   Mary will be able to save money immediately at Jones Engineering because her first year salary is more than $1,800 above the money she needs to pay her bills. At Smithson, her initial salary is $5,000 below the money required to pay her bills. Thus, she will have to use her bonus to break even. The higher percentage of increase at Smithson is not enough to make up the difference.

Step 4   The Smithson starting salary is too far below the Jones starting salary for the extra one percent of increase to make much of a difference. The two salaries after five years are closer than expected because of the second bonus of $5,000 from Smithson.

Step 5   Calculating the math is important to Mary because she might easily be fooled by the higher bonuses at Smithson. Therefore, she might think she will save more at Smithson, even if she realizes the first year loss of $5,000.

Step 6   As a result of completing the math charts, Mary can easily recognize that she can start saving money for her house in the first year if she accepts the position at Jones Engineering.

Because of the length, the student can break the six responses into two paragraphs. Steps one, two and three become one paragraph; the remaining three steps form a second paragraph of the response.

The paragraphs should reveal that the student possesses an understanding of the article at these comprehension levels: literal, synthesis, inferential, evaluative.

Paragraph 1 (steps 1, 2, and 3)

Mary will be able to save $15,000 more by accepting the position at Jones Engineering. At Jones, her yearly salary begins above the $70,000 that she needs to pay for yearly expenses, even with the insurance payment subtracted from her income. At Smithson, Mary will lose $5,000 her first year. She will have to use her bonus to make up the difference. In fact, Mary will lose money in her second year at Smithson, also. Mary will be able to save money immediately at Jones Engineering because her first year salary is more than $1,800 above the money she needs to pay her bills. At Smithson, her initial salary is $5,000 below the money required to pay her bills.   Thus, she will have to use her bonus to break even. The higher percentage of increase at Smithson is not enough to make up the difference.

Paragraph 2 (steps 4, 5, and 6)

The Smithson starting salary is too far below the Jones starting salary for the extra one percentage of increase to make much of a difference. The two salaries after five years are closer than expected because of the second bonus of $5,000 from Smithson. Calculating the math is important to Mary because she might easily be fooled by the higher bonuses at Smithson. Therefore, she might think she will save more at Smithson, even if she realizes the first year loss of $5,000. As a result of completing the math charts, Mary can easily recognize that she can start saving money for her house in the first year if she accepts the position at Jones Engineering.

Teachers can evaluate the six steps of the rough draft according to the rubric on the following page.

Structured Writing Rubric - Math

Student			Teacher		Comment
Yes	No	The main idea is clear.	Yes	No	_____
Yes	No	The "for example" is complete, explaining relevant information and data.	Yes	No	_____
Yes	No	The "why" explains the mathematical reasoning.	Yes	No	_____
Yes	No	The first three parts of the paragraph are logical.	Yes	No	_____
Yes	No	The "why of why" provides additional insight.	Yes	No	_____
Yes	No	The "why important" clearly states the significance of the choice or math step.	Yes	No	_____
Yes	No	Steps in the math process are broken down.	Yes	No	_____
Yes	No	The "as a result" is a logical consequence that relates to the importance.	Yes	No	_____
Yes	No	The entire first draft paragraph is coherent.	Yes	No	_____
Yes	No	The student applies editing and revising skills.	Yes	No	_____

Student Comment: _____

_____

_____

Teacher Comment: _____

_____

_____

Applying the Structured Writing Process

MATHEMATICS

On the pages that follow are several different applications of the Structured Writing process tailored for math classes. Each sample contains the objective or purpose, and a description of the assignment in addition to each of the six steps.

There are two listings for each sample, one contains the student responses for each of the six steps and the second contains the teacher notes for each step. Samples with teacher notes have the words "teacher notes" at the top of the page.

The following are samples for Math classes.

Sample 1:   Persuasive essay

Sample 2:   Expository response

Sample 3:   Response to an article

Sample 4:   Personal narrative

Sample 5:   Response in a business letter

Mathematics – Sample 1	Persuasive Response

Purpose

MAKING ECONOMIC CHOICES
To evaluate which consumer decision is best for specific individual.

Assignment – This is a persuasive response from an Accounting class.

- The response is based on a mathematics problem that focuses on a choice of mortgages.
- The student is given information about one fixed and one adjustable mortgage.
- The student discusses the compulsive spending habits of the friend needing the mortgage.

Step 1: Main Idea

If your goal is to pay off the debt on your house as soon as possible, you are better off choosing the fixed five-year second mortgage for $150,000 rather than the adjustable mortgage beginning at 3.50 percent.

Step 2: For Example

For example, the fixed mortgage will cost you $2,831 per month for five years. The thirty-year mortgage will cost only $674 per month; however, in order to pay off the debt on your house in the five years, you will have to add over $2,000 per month which you can afford.

Step 3: Why

You need to choose the five-year option because of your spending habits that have left you in debt in the past. You have talked with me about how tempted you are to use your charge card, even when you don't really need what you buy. You will not be saving or investing the $2,000.

Step 4: Why of Why

I understand that the five-year fixed mortgage will cost you about $1,800 more in interest per month over the five years. Nevertheless, your past matters, and you need peace of mind.

Step 5: Why Important

Choosing the fixed mortgage is important because it will force you to pay the required amount each month. If you could be sure that you would add enough principle to your monthly payments, you would be better off choosing the adjustable mortgage. However, your past tells me that you should choose the safe route.

Step 6: As a Result

As a result of realizing your past habits, you will have the piece of mind knowing that your house will be totally yours in five years.

Mathematics – Sample 1 (TEACHER'S NOTES)	Persuasive Response

Purpose

MAKING ECONOMIC CHOICES
To evaluate which mortgage terms are best for specific individual.

Assignment – This is a persuasive response from an Accounting class.

- The student's choice makes mathematical sense.
- The student presents mathematical examples that are correct.
- The student embeds mathematical understanding into persuasive text.

Step 1: Main Idea

The sample presents a main idea that identifies the preference of the two choices. The mathematical parameters of each choice are identified by stating the price of the second mortgage and the interest of the adjustable.

Step 2: For Example

The explanation here shows the student's understanding of the monthly cost of the second mortgage and the adjustable (based on the given table). Most significant is the understanding that $2,000 will have to be added to the monthly adjustable payment in order to equal the five-year pay-off.

Step 3: Why

This problem presents information about the obsessive spending habits of the friend and the friend's questionable financial situation. The sentence about the use of the charge card is acceptable literary license.

Step 4: Why of Why

This component presents mathematical information to establish that the writer is empathetic to the friend. Is the greater cost of interest over five years worth the peace of mind?

Step 5: Why Important

This segment shows that the writer understands this choice makes sense for the friend but does not make sense for other consumers. This segment of the response demonstrates an appreciation that the consumer must look at the math in combination with other behaviors.

Step 6: As a Result

The writer presents a consequence of the choice that rounds out the reasoning already stated.

Mathematics – Sample 2	Expository Response

Purpose

THINKING ABOUT PROBLEM SOLVING
To think about the key mathematical principle to keep in mind.

Assignment – This is an expository response concerning geometric shapes.

- The student explains a mathematical problem to determine the amount of carpeting to buy.
- After solving the problem, the student thinks about the most important idea of this problem-solving experience.
- The student understands the perimeter of the room is both rectangular and triangular.

Step 1: Main Idea

The most important idea in order to solve this problem is that I had to figure out the area of the large rectangle and triangles.

Step 2: For Example

For example, the basement needs to be divided into one large rectangle and two triangles. I figured out the areas of the two triangles because I knew the base of each triangle is 20 feet, and the height is 10 feet. I figured out the area of the large rectangle by multiplying the length of 60 feet by the width of 20 feet.

Step 3: Why

I needed to find out the area of two triangles because they are separated by an open space. However, once I knew the area of one triangle, I actually knew the area of the second triangle.

Step 4: Why of Why

The base and height of both triangles are the same; so, I just had to figure out the area of one and double it.

Step 5: Why Important

Finding the areas of the triangles and rectangle is important because I wouldn't want to buy lots of extra carpeting. Suppose I owned the house with this room, and the person I hired charged me for several square yards of extra carpeting. This would cost me lots of extra money if I had not measured the area ahead of time.

Step 6: As a Result

As a result of measuring the dimensions of the basement, I am a well-informed consumer.

Mathematics – Sample 2 (TEACHER'S NOTES)	**Expository Response**

Purpose

THINKING ABOUT PROBLEM SOLVING
To think about the key mathematical principle to keep in mind.

Assignment – This is an expository response concerning geometric shapes.

- The student explains a valid principle that enables him/her to solve the problem.
- The student discusses how this principle allowed him/her to break the problem down into sets of math skills.
- The student presents a practical reason for the application of the principal and the math skills.

Step 1: Main Idea

This response is valid because it shows that the student is centered on the role of the area of geometric shapes to solve the problem. By reflecting on a major principle that was employed in problem solving, the student is required to engage in the meta-cognitive process.

Step 2: For Example

The student explains how he/she arrives at the conclusion expressed in the main idea and why this conclusion works mathematically. The student states the dimensions of one large rectangle, rather than three smaller ones.

Step 3: Why

The student discusses the reason he/she has to deal with two triangles.

Step 4: Why of Why

This explains more about his/her thinking related to the triangles. The student states why there was a need to figure out only one area.

Step 5: Why Important

This statement of application becomes key to a successful response. The student must explain why going through the time of solving a problem like this might be necessary for the consumer. If the student does not appreciate the value of the thinking to real life, the problem-solving process becomes less meaningful.

Step 6: As a Result

This is a simple conclusion that is justified by the previous statement.

Mathematics – Sample 3	**Response Based on an Article**

Purpose

THINKING ABOUT PROBLEM SOLVING
To create a mathematical personal response based on real data.

Assignment – This is a response based on an article related to a current mathematics topic.

- The student reads and discusses an article about acquiring a franchise.
- The student determines which type of franchise he/she what acquire and the monetary investment necessary for the acquisition.
- The student briefly discusses the rate of return based on estimated sales.

Step 1: Main Idea

I would like to purchase the yogurt franchise, even though the initial expense seems quite high.

Step 2: For Example

For example, the total initial investment to qualify for the franchise would be about $230,000. Of this amount, I would have to come up with fifty percent or $115,000; this is the liquid capital. I could borrow the remainder from the yogurt company at an interest rate of 3.5 percent.

Step 3: Why

Before I would invest in this kind of franchise, I need to figure out if I can make enough of a profit. The article states that it would cost me about $4,000 in interest on the loan per year plus $1,500 in principle paid back per month. In addition, there would be about $18,000 in start-up expenses plus another $12,000 per year in other expenses, such as insurance and electricity. With a profit of $0.50 for every dollar received, I would have to decide how much business must take place for the profit.

Step 4: Why of Why

I would need to determine the amount of business because I want to make sure that I am not going to lose my investment.

Step 5: Why Important

Studying the initial expenses is important because I would not want to lose my investment that would have to come from my savings. If the yogurt shop went broke, then I would be broke also.

Step 6: As a Result

As a result of this studying, I would have a good understanding if this investment would be worthwhile.

Mathematics – Sample 3 (TEACHER'S NOTES)	**Response Based on an Article**

Purpose

THINKING ABOUT PROBLEM SOLVING
To create a mathematical personal response based on real data.

Assignment – This is a response based on an article related to a current mathematics topic.

- The student demonstrates literal, synthesis, and inferential comprehension of the article(s).
- The student makes a viable choice based on the data presented.
- The student explains the mathematics necessary to implement selected data and any realistic concerns related to the math.

Step 1: Main Idea

The student could have chosen other discussed franchises. However, he/she selected one, even though there is an evaluative comment about the initial expense. The reader knows that the writer has a concern.

Step 2: For Example

The writer chooses relevant data from the article and presents the data from the article accurately.

Step 3: Why

In this type of response, the "why" component is key. The student is explaining the idea of "why do the math?" He/she explains why there is reason for the concern expressed in the main idea. The student is presenting his/her thinking process for reflecting on relevant data.

Step 4: Why of Why

This sentence shows that an investor in one of these franchises is interested in a profit; losing the investment is a concern.

Step 5: Why Important

This statement is the bottom line. It presents the importance of the student knowing what he/she is doing. This knowledge leads to a well-informed decision. How many financial decisions are made without an adequate level of analysis?

Step 6: As a Result

This final sentence is the logical conclusion. A great deal of length is not necessary because in-depth explanation already has taken place.

Mathematics – Sample 4	Personal Narrative

Purpose

THINKING ABOUT PROBLEM SOLVING
To think about the key mathematical principle to keep in mind.

Assignment – This is a personal narrative based on experience related to the mathematics that did not only involve money.

- The mathematical experience needs to be important to the student.
- The experience needs to solve two or more mathematical operations or processes.
- The student needs to have learned a lesson from the experience.

Step 1: Main Idea

When I was in fifth grade, I really wanted a new baseball glove for the little league season. Unfortunately, I did not have the money to pay for the glove that I wanted.

Step 2: For Example

For example, the glove cost $46.00 plus tax, and I only had $20.00 saved. I needed to find $26.00 plus the 6% tax that came to $2.76.

Step 3: Why

I needed to find a way to get the $28.76 that I was short because the baseball season was only a couple of weeks away. My dad helped me figure out a solution to the problem.

Step 4: Why of Why

My dad told me that he would pay for half of the $28.76 and that he would lend me the rest of the money. I had to pay him back the $14.38 in equal payments over the next year. The $1.10 or $1.09 per month would be deducted from my allowance.

Step 5: Why Important

Finding the money to pay for the baseball glove was important to me because I wound up playing shortstop, and I needed a great glove.

Step 6: As a Result

As a result of getting the glove, I had a terrific season and, even, made the All-Star team.

Mathematics – Sample 4 (TEACHER'S NOTES)   **Personal Narrative**

Purpose

THINKING ABOUT PROBLEM SOLVING
To think about the key mathematical principle to keep in mind.

Assignment – This is a personal narrative based on experience related to the mathematics.

- The mathematical situation as described clearly.
- The mathematical skills are explained, and necessary in-depth processing is included.
- The relevancy of the personal experience is evident.

Step 1: Main Idea

The writer uses two sentences to present the main idea. The first sentence presents the item wanted, and the second sentence presents the reason the item was out of reach.

Step 2: For Example

The math is explained to identify the amount needed, and the amount already saved. The student includes the cost of the 6% tax that is necessary to calculate.

Step 3: Why

The student combines the shortfall from the price with the tax. He, also, presents the idea about the solution to the problem.

Step 4: Why of Why

The writer presents "why" this is the solution. Most significantly, he discusses the financial obligations of the solution. This recognition of obligation strengthens the response.

Step 5: Why Important

Solving the problem is important to the writer because he can succeed in his dream. The financial arrangement with the father allows this to happen. Mathematics plays the key role in arriving at a viable solution.

Step 6: As a Result

This component is the consequence of having the glove.

Mathematics – Sample 5	Business Letter

Purpose

THINKING ABOUT PROBLEM SOLVING
To apply mathematical principles to a real life situation.

Assignment – This is a business letter describing a community concern that involves math.

- The letter is addressed to the mayor or town manager.
- The letter needs to focus on a topic that might be real or developed for this exercise.
- The letter needs to describe the mathematical issue clearly.

Step 1: Main Idea

The high school Social Action Club would like to construct a new wheelchair ramp leading to the rear entrance of the library. Members of the club would work with the town-engineering firm of Jones and Jones in order to construct the ramp according to specifications and with the correct materials.

Step 2: For Example

For example, experts recommend a slope of 1:12 which results in a five degree incline. Since the vertical distance from the ground to the rear entrance door is twelve inches, the ramp constructed will have to be twelve feet long. Mr. Fred Jones, a chief engineer at the firm, will work with us to select the best available materials for the ramp. Mr. Jones and his business partners will pay the cost of these materials.

Step 3: Why

The new ramp will make it easier for the disabled to enter the back entrance of the library. The existing ramp has been closed for nearly a year due to its poor condition.

Step 4: Why of Why

This entrance is adjacent to the parking lot and is much closer than the entrance at the front of the library.

Step 5: Why Important

The construction of this ramp is important to the town because a community goal is to give its residents the best possible quality of life. Some disabled seniors avoid going to the library because they are afraid to walk or ride in their wheelchairs from the parking lot to the front entrance.

Step 6: As a Result

As a result of building this ramp, several people who currently are denied access to the library will have easier access.

Mathematics – Sample 5 (TEACHER'S NOTES)	Business Letter

Purpose

THINKING ABOUT PROBLEM SOLVING
To apply mathematical principles to a real life situation.

Assignment – This is a business letter describing a community concern that involves math.

- The concern is presented clearly with support.
- The mathematical reasoning is stated accurately and significant processing is described.
- The difference resulting from the use of mathematics is clear.

Step 1: Main Idea

The main idea is the construction of the ramp, but the writer includes information about the engineering firm's supporting role because of the technical nature of the work. Immediately, the reader must be confident that the ramp will meet government regulations.

Step 2: For Example

The writer presents mathematical information related to government recommendations. This assures the reader that the student knows what he/she is talking about. Using the mathematical information at this time creates a positive reaction from the reader. The issue of materials is resolved as well.

Step 3: Why

The writer clearly discusses information related to the problem. "Why do we need a new ramp?" This segment presents a clear response.

Step 4: Why of Why

This part of the response supports the "why" section. The combined response to steps 3 and 4 sets up the statement of importance in the next section.

Step 5: Why Important

The first part is an evaluative comment that alludes to a quality of life. The writer is confident that the reader will agree with this assessment. The second part of the response is a clincher based on shared information.

Step 6: As a Result

This conclusion turns the issue into one of basic rights for seniors. The writer can make this bold statement because the previous parts of the response are so strong.

Part 5

Structuring a Personal Narrative Essay

A personal narrative essay is a form of expository writing. The word *expository* means "to explain." The writing of a personal narrative is explaining an event or experience from his or her life.

Writing the Introduction

When teaching students to organize their thinking for the introduction of a personal narrative piece, teachers can follow these simple steps.

Step 1:

The student rephrases the purpose of the prompt. For example, the prompt is as follows:

People depend upon others to provide them with guidance and help during times of need. Tell about one person who has provided you with this guidance and help. Discuss why this person has improved the quality of your life.

The first sentence of the introduction is as follows:

Each of us depends upon a few special people for guidance and help during times of need.

Step 2:

The student indicates the focus for the essay. For example:

Each of us depends upon a few special people for guidance and help during times of need. **One important person who has made a difference in my life is my Uncle Henry.**

The statement of choice restates the main purpose of the prompt while incorporating the focus of the writing. The sentence in the example above does <u>not</u> say: My Uncle Henry helped me. Instead, the second sentence states the following:

One important person who was made a difference in my life is my Uncle Henry.

The words "made a difference" refer back to the prompt.

Step 3:

The student creates a "general" sentence telling about one consequence related to the initial sentence of the introduction and the choice. For example:

Each of us depends upon a few special people for guidance and help during times of need. One important person who has made a difference in my life is my Uncle Henry. **As a result of my Uncle Henry's assistance, the quality of my life has improved significantly.**

This general consequence can begin with the words "as a result," which clue the reader that the sentence is going to express the consequence.

Step 4:

The students state the reasons for their choice of focus. For example:

Each of us depends upon a few special people for guidance and help during times of need. One important person who has made a difference in my life is my Uncle Henry. As a result of my Uncle Henry's assistance, the quality of my life has improved significantly. **My Uncle Henry's value to my life has been demonstrated when he 1) guided me through problems, 2) helped me with my homework, and 3) coached me at sports.**

The numbering of reasons is optional; however, this practice can make it easier for students to remember the main ideas of body paragraphs in the rough draft. The total introduction would read as follows:

Each of us depends upon a few special people for guidance and help during times of need. One important person who has made a difference in my life is my Uncle Henry. As a result of my Uncle Henry's assistance, the quality of my life has improved significantly. My Uncle Henry's value to my life has been demonstrated when he 1) guided me through problems, 2) helped me with my homework, and 3) coached me at sports.

In review, when writing the introduction to a personal narrative essay, the students need to remember these key points.

- ✓ The first sentence rephrases the prompt. However, the students should not merely copy the prompt. They need to modify the language slightly so as to establish personal ownership.

- ✓ The second sentence of the prompt states the focus of the essay. This type of essay has only one focus. For example, the students are not going to write about two different people in the paragraph above. The prompt requires a focus on one person.

- ✓ The general consequence becomes a way to communicate to the reader (or scorer) that the students comprehend the meaning of the prompt. The introduction without this third sentence is weaker.

- ✓ The three reasons stated in the final part of the paragraph are listed. Each reason, usually, begins with the verb. The students should avoid repeating the same verb in the listing. For example, the introduction above expresses three different verbs- "guided," "helped," and "coached."

Teachers can evaluate the introduction of the essay according to the rubric on the next page.

Structured Writing Rubric – Essay Introduction

Student			Teacher		Comment
Yes	**No**	The opening sentence rephrases the prompt.	**Yes**	**No**	_____
Yes	**No**	The second sentence clearly states one focus for the essay.	**Yes**	**No**	_____
Yes	**No**	The first two sentences contain some original language.	**Yes**	**No**	_____
Yes	**No**	The third sentence contains a consequence that indicates the value of the choice.	**Yes**	**No**	_____
Yes	**No**	The reasons are stated clearly.	**Yes**	**No**	_____
Yes	**No**	Sentences contain descriptive language.	**Yes**	**No**	_____
Yes	**No**	Sentences used varying verbs.	**Yes**	**No**	_____
Yes	**No**	The entire paragraph is logical and coherent.	**Yes**	**No**	

Student Comment: _____

_____

_____

Teacher Comment: _____

_____

_____

The First Paragraph in the Body of the Essay

Each paragraph in the body of the essay follows the six-step plan of Structured Writing. These parts are described below.

Step 1:

The student presents their main idea or reason that supports their focus choice. For example:

In the introduction presented during the previous section, the focus choice was Uncle Henry. Therefore, the main idea of this paragraph needs to center around Uncle Henry.

Main Idea   **Uncle Henry was always there to guide me through difficult problems when I was not sure what to do.**

The sentence above presents one reason as to why the author has chosen Uncle Henry as the person who provided guidance. The main idea part of the personal narrative paragraph is usually one lengthy sentence.

Step 2:

The student cites an example that provides specific information about one incident that proves the truth of the main idea statement. For example:

For Example   **For example, when I was in the sixth grade, I had a major argument with my best friend. Uncle Henry spent a long time talking with me about the value of friendship and why it was necessary for my friend and me to try to solve our problem. My friend and I discussed our differences, and we are still friends today.**

Uncle Henry was always there to guide me through difficult problems when I was not sure what to do. **For example, when I was in the sixth grade, I had a major argument with my best friend. Uncle Henry spent a long time talking with me about the** for example value of friendship and why it was necessary for my **friend and me to try to solve our problem. My friend and I discussed our differences, and we are still friends today.**

The "for example" component is an explanation of a situation or event that elaborates on the point in the main idea. This part is often three sentences long. The students do not list several examples. Instead, they elaborate on one meaningful example.

Step 3:

The student discusses "why" the example presented in the second step took place. In this case, the student would respond to the following question.

Question	Why did Uncle Henry want to take the time to help solve the argument?

Why **Uncle Henry understood that friends are not easy to find. He recognized that my friend and I had a strong friendship.**

Uncle Henry was always there to guide me through difficult problems when I was not sure what to do. For example, when I was in the sixth grade, I had a major argument with my best friend. Uncle Henry spent a long time talking with me about the value of friendship and why it was necessary for my friend and me to try to solve our problem. My friend and I discussed our differences, and we are still friends today. **Uncle Henry understood that friends are not easy to find. He recognized that my friend and I had a strong friendship.**

This third part might be two sentences in length. The student needs to make sure that the stated "why" is logical and convincing to the reader.

Step 4:

The student creates a "why of why" statement. This sentence is designed to probe the reason for behavior at a greater depth. In this case, the student would respond to this question based on the sentence in step three.

Question	Why did he want me to know that good friends are not easy to find?

Why of Why **My uncle always thought that people are more important than money. He always told me friends are like gold.**

Uncle Henry was always there to guide me through difficult problems when I was not sure what to do. For example, when I was in the sixth grade, I had a major argument with my best friend. Uncle Henry spent a long time talking with me about the value of friendship and why it was necessary for my friend and me to try to solve our problem. My friend and I discussed our differences, and we are still friends today. Uncle Henry understood that friends are not easy to find. He recognized that my friend and I had a strong friendship. **My uncle always**

thought that people are more important than money. He always told me friends are like gold.

The "why of why" seems difficult at first. However, it is very logical. The student only needs to look at the sentence(s) from step three and formulate a "why" question.

Step 5:

The student responds to a "why important" question. Why is the content of this paragraph important? In this case, the student thinks about the following:

Question	Why is my Uncle's guidance important to me?
Why Important	**My uncle's advice is important to me because he taught me to respect the people who care about me.**

Uncle Henry was always there to guide me through difficult problems when I was not sure what to do. For example, when I was in the sixth grade, I had a major argument with my best friend. Uncle Henry spent a long time talking with me about the value of friendship and why it was necessary for my friend and me to try to solve our problem. My friend and I discussed our differences, and we are still friends today. Uncle Henry understood that friends are not easy to find. He recognized that my friend and I had a strong friendship. My uncle always thought that people are more important than money. He always told me friends are like gold. **My uncle's advice is important to me because he taught me to respect the people who care about me.**

Step 6:

The student concludes the paragraph by writing an "as a result" sentence. This statement ties into the previous step. In this case, the student thinks about the following:

Question	What has been the result of my being able to respect people close to me?
As a Result	**As a result, I have been able to keep up friendships with those people who are significant to my life.**

Uncle Henry was always there to guide me through difficult problems when I was not sure what to do. For example, when I was in the sixth grade, I had a major argument with my best friend. Uncle Henry spent a long time talking with me about the value of friendship and why it was necessary for my friend and me to try to solve our problem. My friend and I discussed our differences, and we are still friends today. Uncle Henry understood that friends are not easy to find. He recognized that my friend and I had a strong friendship. My uncle always thought that people are more important than money. He always told me friends are like gold. My Uncle's advice is important to me because he taught me to respect the people who care about me. **As a result, I have been able to keep up friendships with those people who are significant to my life.**

The first paragraph of the essay body is comprised of these six parts. Steps two through five can be up to three sentences in length.

- the main idea or stated reason
- for example
- why
- why of why
- why important
- as a result

The introduction and the first paragraph in the essay body look like this.

Introduction

Each of us depends upon a few special people for guidance and help during times of need. One important person who has made a difference in my life is my Uncle Henry. As a result of my Uncle Henry's assistance, the quality of my life has improved significantly. My Uncle Henry's value to my life has been demonstrated when he 1) guided me through problems, 2) helped me with my homework, and 3) coached me at sports.

First Paragraph

Uncle Henry was always there to guide me through difficult problems when I was not sure what to do. For example, when I was in the sixth grade, I had a major argument with my best friend. Uncle Henry spent a long time talking with me about the value of friendship and why it was necessary for my friend and me to try to solve our problem. My friend and I discussed our differences, and we are still friends today. Uncle Henry understood that friends are not easy to find. He recognized that my friend and I had a strong friendship. My uncle always thought that people are more important than money. He always told me friends are like gold. My uncle's advice is important to me because he taught me to respect the people who care about me. As a result, I have been able to keep up friendships with those people who are significant to my life.

The Second Paragraph in the Body of the Essay

Step 1:

The student presents their main idea or reason that supports their focus choice. For example:

Main Idea   **Uncle Henry spent a great deal of time helping me with my math homework when I did not understand the problem.**

The sentence above presents a second reason as to why the author has chosen Uncle Henry as a person who provided guidance. In the first main idea, the student used the word "**guide.**" In this main idea, the writer used the word "**help**" for variation.

Step 2:

The student cites an example that provides specific information about one incident that proves the truth of the main idea statement. For example:

For Example   **For example, I became frustrated during one homework assignment on perimeter during seventh grade. I was not sure how to answer several story problems that were due the next day. Uncle Henry sat with me for, at least, two hours showing me how to solve these problems.**

Uncle Henry spent a great deal of time helping me with my math homework when I did not understand what to do. **For example, I became frustrated during one homework assignment on perimeter during seventh grade. I was not sure how to answer several story problems that were due the next day. Uncle Henry sat with me for, at least, two hours showing me how to solve these problems.**

The "for example" component is an explanation of a situation or event that elaborates on the point in the main idea. This part is often three sentences long. The second example cannot be the same or similar to the first example.

Step 3:

The student discusses "why" the example presented in the second step took place. In this case, the student would respond to the following question.

Question   Why did Uncle Henry want to take the time to help me solve the problems?

Why   **Why did Uncle Henry take time to help me solve the problems?**

Uncle Henry spent a great deal of time helping me with my math homework when I did not understand what to do. For example, I became frustrated during one homework assignment on perimeter during seventh grade. I was not sure how to answer several story problems that were due the next day. Uncle Henry sat with me for, at least, two hours showing me how to solve these problems. **He spent this time with me because he wanted me to be successful in school.**

This third part might be two sentences in length. The writer needs to make sure that the stated "why" is logical and convincing to the reader.

Step 4:

The student creates a "why of why" statement. This sentence is designed to probe the reason for behavior at a greater depth. In this case, the student would respond to this question based on the sentence in step three.

Question   Why did he want me to be successful in school?

Why of Why   **Uncle Henry understood that without a good education I would not have very many opportunities.**

Uncle Henry spent a great deal of time helping me with my math homework when I did not understand what to do. For example, I became frustrated during one homework assignment on perimeter during seventh grade. I was not sure how to answer several story problems that were due the next day. Uncle Henry sat with me for, at least, two hours showing me how to solve these problems. He spent this time with me because he wanted me to be successful in school. **Uncle Henry understood that without a good education I would not have very many opportunities.**

Step 5:

The student responds to a "why important" question. Why is the content of this paragraph important? In this case, the student thinks about the following:

Question   Why is my Uncle's help important to me?

Why Important   **Because of my uncle's patience, I have learned not to give up, even when the assignment is difficult.**

Uncle Henry spent a great deal of time helping me with my math homework when I did not understand what to do. For example, I became frustrated during one homework assignment on perimeter during seventh grade. I was not sure how to answer several story problems that were due the next day. Uncle Henry sat with me for, at least, two hours showing me how to solve these problems. He spent this time with me because he wanted me to be successful in school. Uncle Henry understood that without a good education I would not have very many opportunities. **Because of my uncle's patience, I have learned not to give up, even when the assignment is difficult.**

Step 6:

The student concludes the paragraph by writing an "as a result" sentence. This statement ties into the previous step. In this case, the student thinks about the following:

Question   What has been the result of my getting better at solving math problems?

As a Result   **As a result, he gave me the confidence to believe that I could get the right answer.**

Uncle Henry spent a great deal of time helping me with my math homework when I did not understand the problem. For example, I became frustrated during one homework assignment on perimeter during seventh grade. I was not sure how to answer several story problems that were due the next day. Uncle Henry sat with me for, at least, two hours showing me how to solve these problems. He spent this time with me because he wanted me to be successful in school. Uncle Henry understood that without a good education would not have very many opportunities. Because of my uncle's patience, I have learned not to give up, even if the assignment is difficult. **As a result, he gave me the confidence to believe that I could get the right answer.**

The students substitute another word or phrase for "as a result" in revision.

The second paragraph of the essay body is comprised of the same six parts.

- the main idea or stated reason
- for example
- why
- why of why
- why important
- as a result

These body paragraphs are in rough draft form. The students learn to revise and edit.

The introduction and the first two paragraph in the essay body look like this.

Introduction

Each of us depends upon a few special people for guidance and help during times of need. One important person who has made a difference in my life is my Uncle Henry. As a result of my Uncle Henry's assistance, the quality of my life has improved significantly. My Uncle Henry's value to my life has been demonstrated when he 1) guided me through problems, 2) helped me with my homework, and 3) coached me at sports.

First Paragraph

Uncle Henry was always there to guide me through difficult problems when I was not sure what to do. For example, when I was in the sixth grade, I had a major argument with my best friend. Uncle Henry spent a long time talking with me about the value of friendship and why it was necessary for my friend and me to try to solve our problem. My friend and I discussed our differences, and we are still friends today. Uncle Henry understood that friends are not easy to find. He recognized that my friend and I had a strong friendship. My uncle always thought that people are more important than money. He always told me friends are like gold. My Uncle's advice is important to me because he taught me to respect the people who care about me. As a result, I have been able to keep up friendships with those people who are significant to my life.

Second Paragraph

Uncle Henry spent a great deal of time helping me with my math homework when I did not understand what to do. For example, I became frustrated during one homework assignment on perimeter during seventh grade. I was not sure how to answer several story problems that were due the next day. Uncle Henry sat with me for, at least, two hours showing me how to solve these problems. He spent this time with me because he wanted me to be successful in school. Uncle Henry understood that without a good education I would not have very many opportunities. Because of my uncle's patience, I learned not to give up, even if the assignment is difficult. As a result, he gave me the confidence to believe that I could get the right answer.

The Third Paragraph in the Body of the Essay

Step 1:

The student presents the main idea or reason that supports their focus choice. For example:

Main Idea   **My Uncle Henry is also special to me because he showed me how to be a better athlete.**

Step 2:

The student cites an example that provides specific information about one incident that proves the truth of the main idea statement. For example:

For Example   **For example, when I was eight years old, I joined a little league team. I had a lot of trouble figuring out how to hit, and my uncle worked with me for three or four weeks. He taught me how to square off on the ball and how to move my feet like I was squishing a bug.**

My Uncle Henry is also special to me because he showed me how to be a better athlete. **For example, when I was eight years old, I joined a little league team. I had a lot of trouble figuring out how to hit, and my uncle worked with me for three or four weeks. He taught me how to square off on the ball and how to move my feet like I was squishing a bug.**

Step 3:

The student discusses "why" the example presented in the second step took place. In this case, the student would respond to the following question.

Question   Why did Uncle Henry want to take the time to teach me to hit?

Why   **My uncle could see that I was getting depressed every time I struck out. He wanted me to feel good about myself.**

My Uncle Henry is also special to me because he showed me how to be a better athlete. For example, when I was eight years old, I joined a little league team. I had a lot of trouble figuring out how to hit, and my uncle worked with me for three or four weeks. He taught me how to square off on the ball and how to move my feet like I was squishing a bug. **My uncle could see that I was getting depressed every time I struck out. He wanted me to feel good about myself.**

Step 4:

The student creates a "why of why" statement. In this case, the student would respond to this question based on the sentence in step three.

Question	Why did he want me to feel good about myself?
Why of Why	**Uncle Henry loved sports, and he wanted me to enjoy them, too.**

My Uncle Henry is also special to me because he showed me how to be a better athlete. For example, when I was eight years old, I joined a little league team. I had a lot of trouble figuring out how to hit, and my uncle worked with me for three or four weeks. He taught me how to square off on the ball and how to move my feet like I was squishing a bug. My uncle could see that I was getting depressed every time I struck out. He wanted me to feel good about myself. **Uncle Henry loved sports, and he wanted me to enjoy them, too.**

Step 5:

The student responds to a "why important" question. Why is the content of this paragraph important? In this case, the student thinks about the following:

Question	Why is my Uncle's help important to me?
Why Important	**I never would have learned to hit a pitched baseball if it had not been for Uncle Henry's willingness to help.**

My Uncle Henry is also special to me because he showed me how to be a better athlete. For example, when I was eight years old, I joined a little league team. I had a lot of trouble figuring out how to hit, and my uncle worked with me for three or four weeks. He taught me how to square off on the ball and how to move my feet like I was squishing a bug. My uncle could see that I was getting depressed every time I struck out. He wanted me to feel good about myself. Uncle Henry loved sports, and he wanted me to enjoy them, too. **I never would have learned to hit a pitched baseball if it had not been for Uncle Henry's willingness to help.**

Step 6:

The student concludes the paragraph by writing an "as a result" sentence. This statement ties into the previous step. In this case, the student thinks about the following:

Question	What has been the result of my getting better at hitting?
As a Result	**As a result of his instruction, I went on to hit for an average of over .300 during that season when I was eight-years old.**

My Uncle Henry is also special to me because he showed me how to be a better athlete. For example, when I was eight years old, I joined a little league team. I had a lot of trouble figuring out how to hit, and my uncle worked with me for three or four weeks. He taught me how to square off on the ball and how to move my feet like I was squishing a bug. My uncle could see that I was getting depressed every time I struck out. He wanted me to feel good about myself. Uncle Henry loved sports, and he wanted me to enjoy them, too. I never would have learned to hit a pitched baseball if it had not been for Uncle Henry's willingness to help. **As a result of his instruction, I went on to hit for an average of over .300 during that season when I was eight-years old.**

The students substitute another word or phrase for "as a result" in revision.

The third paragraph of the essay body is comprised of the same six parts.

- the main idea or stated reason
- for example
- why
- why of why
- why important
- as a result

The introduction and the first three paragraph in the essay body look like this.

Introduction

Each of us depends upon a few special people for guidance and help during times of need. One important person who has made a difference in my life is my Uncle Henry. As a result of my Uncle Henry's assistance, the quality of my life has improved significantly. My Uncle Henry's value to my life has been demonstrated when he 1) guided me through problems, 2) helped me with my homework, and 3) coached me at sports.

First Paragraph

Uncle Henry was always there to guide me through difficult problems when I was not sure what to do. For example, when I was in the sixth grade, I had a major argument with my best friend. Uncle Henry spent a long time talking with me about the value of friendship and why it was necessary for my friend and me to try to solve our problem. My friend and I discussed our differences, and we are still friends today. Uncle Henry understood that friends are not easy to find. He recognized that my friend and I had a strong friendship. My uncle always thought that people are more important than money. He always told me friends are like gold. My Uncle's advice is important to me because he taught me to respect the people who care about me. As a result, I have been able to keep up friendships with those people who are significant to my life.

Second Paragraph

Uncle Henry spent a great deal of time helping me with my math homework when I did not understand what to do. For example, I became frustrated during one homework assignment on perimeter during seventh grade. I was not sure how to answer several story problems that were due the next day. Uncle Henry sat with me for, at least, two hours showing me how to solve these problems. He spent this time with me because he wanted me to be successful in school. Uncle Henry understood that without a good education I would not have very many opportunities. Because of my uncle's patience, I learned not to give up, even if the assignment is difficult. As a result, he gave me the confidence to believe that I could get the right answer.

Third Paragraph

My Uncle Henry is also special to me because he showed me how to be a better athlete. For example, when I was eight years old, I joined a little league team. I had a lot of trouble figuring out how to hit, and my uncle worked with me for three or four weeks. He taught me how to square off on the ball and how to move my feet like I was squishing a bug. My uncle could see that I was getting depressed every time I struck out. He wanted me to feel good about myself. Uncle Henry loved sports, and he wanted me to enjoy them, too. I never would have learned to hit a pitched baseball if it had not been for Henry's willingness to help. As a result of his instruction, I went on to hit for an average of over .300 during that season when I was eight-years old.

Teachers can evaluate each body paragraph of the essay according to the rubric on the following page.

Structured Writing Rubric – Essay Body Paragraphs

Student			Teacher		Comment
Yes	No	The opening sentence statement is clear.	Yes	No	_____
Yes	No	The "for example" is complete, explaining one event or situation.	Yes	No	_____
Yes	No	The "why" explains the cause of the action discussed in the example.	Yes	No	_____
Yes	No	The first three parts of the paragraph are logical.	Yes	No	_____
Yes	No	The "why of why" provides additional insight.	Yes	No	_____
Yes	No	The "why important" clearly states the significance.	Yes	No	_____
Yes	No	The action of the event is broken down.	Yes	No	_____
Yes	No	The "as a result" is the logical consequence that relates the importance.	Yes	No	_____
Yes	No	The entire first draft paragraph is coherent.	Yes	No	_____
Yes	No	The student applies to editing and revising skills	Yes	No	_____

Student Comment: _____

_____

_____

Teacher Comment: _____

_____

_____

The Conclusion of the Essay

The student follows three basic steps to compose the conclusion of the essay in the rough draft.

Step 1:

The student restates the purpose of the prompt, combining sentences one and two from the introduction. The first two sentences of the **introduction** are as follows:

> Each of us depends upon a few special people for guidance and help during times of me. One important person who made a difference in my life is my Uncle Henry.

The first sentence of the conclusion is as follows:

> **My Uncle Henry is a special person who has provided me with guidance and help during times of need.**

Step 2:

The student generates a sentence based on the "as a result" sentences of the three body paragraphs. The three "as a result" sentences **from the body paragraphs** are as follows:

> As a result, I have been able to keep up friendships with those people who are significant to my life.

> He gave me the confidence to believe that I could get the right answer.

> As a result of his instruction, I went on to hit for an average of over .300 during that season when I was eight.

The second sentence of this conclusion is as follows:

> **He has taught me about friendships, given me self-confidence, and, even, made me a better athlete.**

Step 3:

The final sentence of the conclusion sends a message to the reader about the overall purpose of the essay. For example:

> **My uncle is one of the most important people in my life, and I wish all my friends could have someone like him in their family.**

The conclusion looks like this.

My Uncle Henry is a special person who has provided me with guidance and help during my times of need. He has taught me about friendships, given me self-confidence, and, even, made me a better athlete. My uncle is one of the most important people in my life, and I wish all my friends could have someone like him in their family.

The entire essay looks like this.

Introduction

Each of us depends upon a few special people for guidance and help during times of need. One important person who has made a difference in my life is my Uncle Henry. As a result of my Uncle Henry's assistance, the quality of my life has improved significantly. My Uncle Henry's value to my life has been demonstrated when he 1) guided me through problems, 2) helped me with my homework, and 3) coached me at sports.

First Paragraph

Uncle Henry was always there to guide me through difficult problems when I was not sure what to do. For example, when I was in the sixth grade, I had a major argument with my best friend. Uncle Henry spent a long time talking with me about the value of friendship and why it was necessary for my friend and me to try to solve our problem. My friend and I discussed our differences, and we are still friends today. Uncle Henry understood that friends are not easy to find. He recognized that my friend and I had a strong friendship. My uncle always thought that people are more important than money. He always told me friends are like gold. My uncle's advice is important to me because he taught me to respect the people who care about me. As a result, I have been able to keep up friendships with those people who are significant to my life.

Second Paragraph

Uncle Henry spent a great deal of time helping me with my math homework when I did not understand what to do. For example, I became frustrated during one homework assignment on perimeter during seventh grade. I was not sure how to answer several story problems that were due the next day. Uncle Henry sat with me for, at least, two hours showing me how to solve these problems. He spent this time with me because he wanted me to be successful in school. Uncle Henry understood that without a good education I would not have very many opportunities. Because of my uncle's patience, I learned not to give up, even if the assignment is difficult. As a result, he gave me the confidence to believe that I could get the right answer.

Third Paragraph

My Uncle Henry is also special to me because he showed me how to be a better athlete. For example, when I was eight years old, I joined a little league team. I had a lot of trouble figuring out how to hit, and my uncle worked with me for three or four weeks. He taught me how to square off on the ball and how to move my feet like I was squishing a bug. My uncle could see that I was getting depressed every time I struck out. He wanted me to feel good about myself. Uncle Henry loved sports, and he wanted me to enjoy them, too. I never would have learned to hit a pitched baseball if it had not been for Henry's willingness to help. As a result of his instruction, I went on to hit for an average of over .300 during that season when I was eight-years old.

Conclusion

My Uncle Henry is a special person who has provided me with guidance and help during my times of need. He has taught me about friendships, given me self-confidence, and, even, made me a better athlete. My uncle is one of the most important people in my life, and I wish all my friends could have someone like him in their family.

Appendices

Structured Writing Rubric - English

Student			Teacher		Comment
Yes	No	The main idea is clear.	Yes	No	_____
Yes	No	The "for example" is complete, explaining one event or situation.	Yes	No	_____
Yes	No	The "why" explains the cause of the action discussed in the example.	Yes	No	_____
Yes	No	The first three parts of the paragraph are logical.	Yes	No	_____
Yes	No	The "why of why" provides additional insight.	Yes	No	_____
Yes	No	The "why important" clearly states the significance	Yes	No	_____
Yes	No	The action of the event is broken down.	Yes	No	_____
Yes	No	The "as a result" is a logical consequence that relates to the importance.	Yes	No	_____
Yes	No	The entire first draft paragraph is coherent.	Yes	No	_____
Yes	No	The student applies editing and revising skills.	Yes	No	_____

Student Comment: _____

_____

_____

Teacher Comment: _____

_____

_____

Structured Writing Rubric - Science

Student			Teacher		Comment
Yes	No	The main idea is clear.	Yes	No	_____
Yes	No	The "for example" is complete, explaining one event or situation.	Yes	No	_____
Yes	No	The "why" explains the cause of the action discussed in the example.	Yes	No	_____
Yes	No	The first three parts of the paragraph are logical.	Yes	No	_____
Yes	No	The "why of why" provides additional insight.	Yes	No	_____
Yes	No	The "why important" clearly states the significance	Yes	No	_____
Yes	No	The meaning of the information is broken down.	Yes	No	_____
Yes	No	The "as a result" is a logical consequence that relates to the importance.	Yes	No	_____
Yes	No	The entire first draft paragraph is coherent.	Yes	No	_____
Yes	No	The student applies editing and revising skills.	Yes	No	_____

Student Comment: _____

_____

_____

Teacher Comment: _____

_____

_____

Structured Writing Rubric – Social Studies

Student			Teacher		Comment
Yes	No	The main idea is clear.	Yes	No	_____
Yes	No	The "for example" is complete, explaining one event or situation.	Yes	No	_____
Yes	No	The "why" explains the cause of the action discussed in the example.	Yes	No	_____
Yes	No	The first three parts of the paragraph are logical.	Yes	No	_____
Yes	No	The "why of why" provides additional insight.	Yes	No	_____
Yes	No	The "why important" clearly states the significance.	Yes	No	_____
Yes	No	The action of the event is broken down.	Yes	No	_____
Yes	No	The "as a result" is a logical consequence that relates to the importance.	Yes	No	_____
Yes	No	The entire first draft paragraph is coherent.	Yes	No	_____
Yes	No	The student applies editing and revising skills.	Yes	No	_____

Student Comment: _____

_____

_____

Teacher Comment: _____

_____

_____

Structured Writing Rubric - Math

Student			Teacher		Comment
Yes	No	The main idea is clear.	Yes	No	_____
Yes	No	The "for example" is complete, explaining relevant information and data.	Yes	No	_____
Yes	No	The "why" explains the mathematical reasoning.	Yes	No	_____
Yes	No	The first three parts of the paragraph are logical.	Yes	No	_____
Yes	No	The "why of why" provides additional insight.	Yes	No	_____
Yes	No	The "why important" clearly states the significance of the choice or math step.	Yes	No	_____
Yes	No	Steps in the math process are broken down.	Yes	No	_____
Yes	No	The "as a result" is a logical consequence that relates to the importance.	Yes	No	_____
Yes	No	The entire first draft paragraph is coherent.	Yes	No	_____
Yes	No	The student applies editing and revising skills.	Yes	No	_____

Student Comment: _____

_____

Teacher Comment: _____

_____

Structured Writing Rubric – Essay Introduction

Student			Teacher		Comment
Yes	No	The opening sentence rephrases the prompt.	Yes	No	_____
Yes	No	The second sentence clearly states one focus for the essay.	Yes	No	_____
Yes	No	The first two sentences contain some original language.	Yes	No	_____
Yes	No	The third sentence contains a consequence that indicates the value of the choice.	Yes	No	_____
Yes	No	The reasons are stated clearly.	Yes	No	_____
Yes	No	Sentences contain descriptive language.	Yes	No	_____
Yes	No	Sentences used varying verbs.	Yes	No	_____
Yes	No	The entire paragraph is logical and coherent.	Yes	No	

Student Comment: _____

_____

_____

Teacher Comment: _____

_____

_____

Structured Writing Rubric – Essay Body Paragraphs

Student			Teacher		Comment
Yes	No	The opening sentence statement is clear.	Yes	No	_____
Yes	No	The "for example" is complete, explaining one event or situation.	Yes	No	_____
Yes	No	The "why" explains the cause of the action discussed in the example.	Yes	No	_____
Yes	No	The first three parts of the paragraph are logical.	Yes	No	_____
Yes	No	The "why of why" provides additional insight.	Yes	No	_____
Yes	No	The "why important" clearly states the significance.	Yes	No	_____
Yes	No	The action of the event is broken down.	Yes	No	_____
Yes	No	The "as a result" is the logical consequence that relates the importance.	Yes	No	_____
Yes	No	The entire first draft paragraph is coherent.	Yes	No	_____
Yes	No	The student applies to editing and revising skills	Yes	No	_____

Student Comment: _____

_____

_____

Teacher Comment: _____

_____

_____

Made in the USA
Middletown, DE
22 March 2024

51498032R00082